Mark and Gus

Frank S. Anthony

Cover artwork - Jorge Pacheco

© 2011 A G Books

© 2011 A G Books

All rights reserved. No part of this electronic work covered by copyright may be reproduced, copied, or transmitted in any form or by any means (including graphic, electronic or mechanical, photocopying, recording, recording taping, or information retrievable systems) without the prior written permission of the copyright owner.

Mark and Gus
Author - Frank S. Anthony

Published by AG Books New Zealand 2012
24 Harper St
Wanganui, New Zealand

ISBN 978-0-473-21003-8

Visit our website for more great classic New Zealand ebooks at – http://www.agbooks.co.nz/

Foreword

Frank Sheldon Anthony's "Me and Gus" became immortalized on New Zealand radio in the 1950s. His characters, Gus and Mark, are two of the most well-recognized in New Zealand fiction. Anthony is one of New Zealand's most prominent comic fiction writers. He was one of the first authors to feature everyday life in rural New Zealand using a distinctly New Zealand dialect.

Frank Sheldon Anthony was born in Makaraka near Gisborne on the 13th of December, 1891. His father Frank Anthony Senior, received remittances from his family in England and dabbled in various types of work. Anthony's mother Annie, (born McGlashan) was a governess and schoolteacher before marriage and became a schoolteacher for the Whakamara Primary School. Anthony had one older sister and two younger sisters, who all became schoolteachers.

In the 1890s the Anthonys lived in various places in South Taranaki. Anthony's father owned hotels for short periods in Hawera and Manutahi. He also owned racehorses.

In 1902 the family settled in Whakamara, a remote settlement near Hawera and Manutahi. Anthony completed primary school, probably under the tutelage of his mother, and attended Hawera District high school in 1905.

It was during that time — with the encouragement of his mother — that he filled notebooks with poems and stories. These were mostly accounts of everyday happenings in a style similar to Mark Twain — one of Anthony's favourite authors. After 2 years of high school, Anthony left to work a year as a farm hand, but in 1909 he decided to go to sea. He was 17 years old.

Anthony worked the next 8 years at sea. First as a deck hand on a few coastal steamers and then on merchant sailing vessels. When the First World War started in 1914, Anthony joined the Royal Navy. He became a gunner on the destroyer ship *Opal*. The *Opal* was based in the North Sea and was involved in the Battle of Jutland.

In 1916, Anthony was attaching the ship to a buoy when he was crushed between them. He suffered a permanent lung injury, an injury which made him susceptible to consumption for the rest of his life. In 1918, Anthony was repatriated to New Zealand and spent several months in Te Waikato Sanatorium in Cambridge before he returned to Taranaki.

He received a British naval pension of 26 shillings and sixpence a week. The soldiers rehabilitation grant loaned him some money to buy land, but the soaring prices of farmland in Taranaki at the time made this difficult. He finally purchased 76 acres of substandard land on Denbigh Road, Midhirst near Stratford in 1919. The farm was very similar to the farm that his narrator describes in the story *Some Pioneering*.

He tried for 5 years to create a working dairy farm and repay his mortgage, but the boulders, tree stumps and swamp as well as his health barely allowed him to feed the 17 or 18 dairy cows that he owned. In 1922, possibly to entertain himself during his lonely winter nights in his shack, he began to write again.

Drawing from the experiences of his life on a struggling dairy farm, he created a series of comic short stories. Ten of these were published from 23rd of June, 1923 to 24th of August, 1924 in the *Auckland Weekly News*, *New Zealand Herald* and the *Christchurch Weekly Press*. He became a prolific writer and had written three completed novels and two unfinished ones during this time. Two of his novels, *Follow the Call* and *Windjammer Sailors* were also serialised and published in the *Christchurch Weekly Press*.

With these small successes under his belt, Anthony began to dream about a career as a novelist. He sold the farm in late 1924 and went to chase the dream that captivate many New Zealand authors. He went to England to pursue a more lucrative career in writing. The writing dream was probably not the only reason he went to England as he was hoping to persuade Phyllis Symonds, a Taranaki woman, to marry him. His unfinished novel *The Girl* was based on his relationship with Symonds. Symonds was on a working holiday in England at the time. Unfortunately for Anthony, she was not interested and only saw him as a friendly acquaintance.

Anthony diligently began working on his writing. He revised *Follow the Call* and *Windjammer Sailors*, toning down the New Zealand vernacular to make it more suitable for a British audience. He also expanded his short stories from the *Gus and Me* serials to create the novel *Gus Tomlins*. He wrote and submitted short stories based on his life at sea. He also wrote *A Cog in the Wheel*, a novel about his time on the *Opal* and *Joe West A.B.*

None of his work was published and when Phyllis Symonds returned in 1926, Anthony was living a life of isolation, frequently moving from boarding-house to boarding-house. His health was deteriorating and the English winters exacerbated his lung injury. Anthony died alone in a boarding-house in Bascombe near Bournemouth on the 13th of January, 1927. He was 35 years old.

Two of Anthony's sea-faring stories were published by British magazines after his death. None of his work was published in book form during his lifetime. His mother collected his writing

Mark and Gus

and arranged to have *Follow the Call* and *Me and Gus* published in 1936 and 1938 respectively. In the 1950s Anthony's mother also came in contact with Francis Jackson, who adapted Anthony's work for radio. The novel *Gus Tomlins* was published in 1977 for the first time.

What is unique about Anthony's work is his satirical accounts of rural New Zealand life after World War I. Anthony's writing uses New Zealand idioms, markedly masculine experiences and a deadpan delivery which make his stories a comic masterpiece. This innovative style was further built on by Frank Sageson and John Mulgan in later years.

Even now, many New Zealanders will be able to relate to situations — though probably not to the absurd extent — in which Gus and Mark find themselves. Anthony excelled at interpreting the life of New Zealand dairy farmers.
The authenticity that he wrote with could only be done by a man who has "lived the life" himself.
Mark, the narrator in these stories gives what he believes is a dispassionate account of the story at hand, ironically failing to realize his own part in how everything turns out.

We have a perfect comic foil in Gus and Mark. Gus being the exuberant extrovert, who is the spark for the comic situation; embodied by his feisty motorcycle and side-car and Mark, sure, steady and a bit slow with his gig trying to sort out the mess that Gus has made.

The farm animals become important supporting characters and in *My New Heifer* and *Gus Buys a Horse*, they steal the show with their distinct personalities. Anthony also illustrates a life that is decidedly masculine, with commentaries on their housekeeping skills in *Gus Buys a Bull* as well as the shoddy attempts at courtship in *Gus and His Girl* and *Violet Again*.

As a writer in New Zealand Anthony was isolated, subjected to pressures of weekly journalism and had difficulty finding a publisher for his novels. He also wrote at a time when the preferred style of stories and novels was escapism and light entertainment.

E.H. McCormick describes Anthony as a writer who "effected during the early twenties a minor revolution in New Zealand fiction". He created a genuine folk image of New Zealanders; an image which many Kiwis resonated with. The matter-of-fact tone of his narratives in contrast to the world of confusion his characters face makes his farcical tales a delight to read.

This book, *Mark and Gus*, is an anthology of Anthony's original 10 stories as they appeared in the newspapers between 1923-1924. In editing these stories for a modern audience, small changes have been made to the text. These are mostly the correction of spelling, print and punctuation errors. Capitalisations and hyphenation have been regularised e.g. 'to-day' has been changed to 'today'; 'Gus'' has been changed to 'Gus's' and 'alright' has been changed to 'all right'. It was a privilege to have edited stories which portray a slice of New Zealand history and culture and I hope that you get as much enjoyment from reading them as I have.

L. Gosyne

Mark and Gus

Contents

Some Pioneering	1
My New Heifer	5
Helping Out Gus	12
Gus Buys a Horse	19
Wood-Splitting with Gus	25
Our Quiet Winter	31
Gus and His Girl	41
Gus Buys a Bull	49
Violet Again	59
Mowing Our Hay	68

Mark and Gus

Some Pioneering

Not everyone has a farm like mine! This is a good job really, because I don't think everyone could farm my class of land and I'm quite sure everyone couldn't live on the returns from it.

It's a beautiful place. There is one little hill near the house. The rest is perfectly flat rimu and white pine swamp. The hill comes in handy to keep the herd on when the swamps are under water. I can feed them on hay there until the floods abate.

I will admit that when I bought this place, I was a new chum. The land agent who took me over the place laid particular stress on the beautiful flat swamps. He said drained swamps were proving to be the most fertile lands in the Dominion. "Look at the Piako Swamp," he said.

A fellow had told me only the week before that he grew parsnips in the Piako one year; 7 feet long. So I decided to take the place.

As soon as I was settled properly, I wired in to the driest part of the swamp intending to drain it. Only there didn't happen to be any outlet for the water unless I opened up a drain for miles. So I started stumping instead. Three months of galling toil saw me with about two acres partly cleared up. I went to town, bought a nice light plough and decided to plough it. I had a theory that a light plough would be easier for the horses to pull than a heavier make. I had never done any ploughing but a young and enthusiastic cousin of mine, who happened along on a visit, decided to stop and see me through the first day. He had done miles and miles of ploughing down on the plains somewhere or other.

As soon as my nice, fat, lazy horses got on to that paddock, the fun commenced. One would suppose I was asking them to plough a bottomless morass, the fuss they made. I knew they couldn't sink down more than a few feet because during stumping operations I had gone probing about with a crowbar, and had located a hidden forest just under the one on top. I remember thinking at the time what a good job it was there, as it would prevent stock getting bogged very deep in wet weather. I tried making the horses stand in one place until they sunk down on to it. I thought that would restore their confidence but it was no go. So we decided to start ploughing and take some of the freshness out of them with hard work.

The young cousin had brought over a bottle of beer with him. We thought we would do things properly, so we cracked the top off the bottle and christened the plough 'Endeavour'. I picked that name. It seemed fitting and rather touching. You know the idea — green fields from barren waste — turning over the virgin soil — exploring the unknown!

Then we started. I held the handles and my cousin drove the horses. First time round the two acres was a bit of an eye-opener to me. We did it in a few seconds and when we came to a stop on a dry spot near the gate, the cousin came to light with a suggestion. He thought we should re-christen the Endeavour and call her the Swallow. He said she was in the air most of the time, and skimmed the little she did plough, and if that was the way she was going to work, his name was the most appropriate. However, I pointed out that she endeavoured to plough a little here and there, and perhaps he hadn't set her quite right. So he got the spanner, gave her more depth, and we started again.

We certainly didn't skim after that. The Endeavour took the earth and started to turn a wet and sticky furrow a foot to eighteen inches deep. This seemed to put the horses on their mettle, and we did slightly better this time round than the first go. I remember, as I sailed round that paddock with my feet just touching ground here and there, thinking high and noble thoughts, like carving a home in the wilderness, and not turning back once my hand was put to the plough. I felt a thrill of pity for the old men, the city dudes, and all those who earned a nice easy living somewhere, because they were not game to come into the back blocks and live a man's life. I had it pretty bad. Everytime we came to the dry patch near the gate we had a spell. We needed it too, but we called it 'resting the horses'.

Some Pioneering

The fourth time round promised to be even quicker than the others. We started off by striking a root which by some carelessness on my part, had not been taken out when I stumped the piece. The Endeavour creaked, the horses sank and snorted. Just when things began to look really serious — I thought I was going to lose my team — the root broke with a snap and the ploughing operations commenced again with considerable vim. The horses tore round that paddock as if it were coated with thin ice, and I may say here that about this part of the proceedings, I began to get the breeze up. It seemed to me that there was more in ploughing a wet swamp than one would first suppose.

I glanced at the cousin. He was doing a steady lope beside the plough, the reins half dragging him along. He seemed to be rather enjoying himself. I thought it would be a good plan next time we stopped to let him have a turn at the handles for a bit, while I drove. To anyone knowing little about the noble art of ploughing, I might explain that when a single furrow plough, travelling at several miles an hour, hits a solid obstacle, like a root or stump, the jar is pretty considerable and communicates itself to the man on the handles in no uncertain manner.

The young cousin didn't seem to mind how much I got jarred. In fact I caught him once flicking old Bloss with the rein when she seemed inclined to ease up on a dry patch of the paddock. I hadn't time to remonstrate because she bounded forward and just about then we (Endeavour and me) struck that dry spot. I investigated afterwards and found it to be a submerged rata tree, 6 feet through and about 60 feet long. The plough shot straight up in the air, hovered for a bit, and then fell on me, removing a piece of scalp 2 inches by 2 and a half inches.

After the young cousin had brought me to by sprinkling me with green swamp water, we had a look round. The old Endeavour was piled up in a most hopeless way. Her bow and cable gear were torn clean off, and we couldn't try to fit them on again because the horses had gone home with them. The beam was bent; the coulter buckled. A lot of other little things we didn't know the names of were broken or twisted so I thought I wouldn't do any more ploughing that day.

We decided to go home. The track back was strewn with chains, swinglebars and other gear, and we found the horses on the top of the little hill near the house. They were milling round, snorting and kicking at all the chains and things they hadn't shed on the homeward sprint. We had considerable difficulty in quieting them sufficiently to get them untangled. They seem to think that if they stood still a second the hill might dissolve under their feet. Both of them were lame, and it was three days before they bucked up sufficiently to hobble off that knoll and look for nourishment in the swamp again.

I had to borrow a horse from a neighbour to run my milk to the factory. He said he would lend me a horse, but I wasn't to use him for ploughing as he was too fast. I agreed to that. Ploughing with fast horses makes my head ache anyway. The young cousin went home next day and the Endeavour is still over the paddock, stuck in that rata log. Some day I hope the young cousin will pay me another visit. When he does, I am going to salve that old derelict, get her patched up at the blacksmith's and finish ploughing that two acres. I shall drive the horses and he can have the handles.

My New Heifer

A fellow sold me a heifer one year. He said she was a well-bred little thing; all she wanted was gentle handling, and she would probably be the best cow in my herd. He said if I cared to take her, he would pop her in at my gate straight away as he had her out on the road.

I was short that spring, so I snapped the offer, and went out on to the road to help him turn her in. Right from the start that heifer looked scary to me, and before we got her on to my farm she had jumped three fences, and led us a dance over about four miles of country.

The owner said it was only to be expected because he had mustered her up with the dogs that morning, and of course she was excited and upset. I think now that the reason I got a cheap heifer that morning was because he had made up his mind that he could never get her as far as the sale-yards, but he never mentioned anything like that to me. He suggested that if I kept her about the sheds for a day or two, and hand-fed her on hay, she would calm down, and follow me about like a dog. I tried that the same afternoon. I noticed that as soon as I got anywhere within a hundred yards of her, she would start to circle round, and eye weak spots in the fence. So I used a little tact, and finally got her penned up in the stock-yard. Then I went to the hay-shed, and got a big armful of hay. I threw it over the rails of the yard, and gave my new purchase such a fright that she got her head stuck between two of the fence rails, and nearly broke her neck. By the time she had cleared herself, I was over the rails, and advancing on her with the hay in my arms again.

The man made a bit of a mistake in his calculations, or else I misunderstood him, because she certainly followed me round — but not like a dog. Unless he meant a mad dog, and I don't think that's what he said. I had to hurry myself a little in order to get over the fence before she got me. Then, I sat on the top rail for a few minutes, and watched her tear that heap of hay into single straws and trample on each one separately. That set me thinking, and I decided to leave her to it for a while and try her again when she was hungry.

The next time I tried to feed her, I lowered the hay over the rails on a long pole, but my dog went into the yard to inspect an old bone there and spoilt things. He didn't stop there very long, and the heifer knocked off a horn showing him the way out, and both of them got excited about it. I tied the dog up for my next attempt, and tried her with a few swedes instead of the hay. Every time I threw a swede over, she jumped at a fresh part of the fence. Then an old cove from Close Handy happened to drop in and said, "What's the use of doing that? Can't you see the heifer's frightened of you? Take her quietly man, take her quietly."

He said it was a strange sort of heifer that could beat him, and he'd show me how to work things.

He took a short stick in one hand and a wisp of hay in the other, and climbed down into the yard. Then he said, "Watch me," and advanced on the heifer.

I must say, that for an old man, he was worth watching.

As I told him, it was as pretty an exhibition of aerial acrobatics as I have seen for a long time.

I think my performance was a trifle better, because I had two horns to side step, while I have an idea that the absence of a horn saved that old chap from a very unpleasant experience. When he was firmly planted on the top rail of the yard he started to say some things about it. Why hadn't I told him she was like that? I was the sort of person who would let a man go to certain death sooner than say a word in warning.

Then when I saw a man mangled to death he supposed I'd laugh.

Well, he'd come over to give me a hand, but in future I could do my own dirty work. He called in at my house as he went away, and borrowed my saddle and bridle. I have an idea that he really came over for them, but whichever it was, he never

My New Heifer

stopped to help me any more. I sat on the rail and admired the latest acquisition to my herd for a while, and then opened the gate and let her out with the other cows.

I was feeding out hay at the time, and everyday I used to cart a load out and fork it about the paddock. While I was busy doing this my old cows used to gather round, get in front of the horse and chase each other for tasty tit-bits, and kick up a deuce of a row.

My new heifer would occupy the time in trotting up and down the furthest fence, waiting for me to go away. When I was well clear of the paddock she would circle round the feeding herd, in ever diminishing circles, and by the time they had cleared up all the hay she would arrive at the outer edge of the feeding area, and start looking hungry. There wasn't much grass anywhere at that time, and I began to feel anxious, because she was going down in condition.

Then one morning I went out, and found her trotting about with a calf nearly as active as herself. This was where the real business began, because somehow or other I had to inveigle that heifer into the cow shed, milk her, and capture the calf. I wasn't in love with the idea at all, but it had to be done. I refused to be enticed more than a chain away from the fence when I sallied forth to bring her home, but I needn't have worried myself.

As soon as she set eyes on me she went off like a shot, and left me to capture the calf without any interference. The calf took after its parent, and went off like a packet of crackers as soon as I clapped my hands on it. I had it jammed in a corner, and when it found there was no escape it turned round and charged, like an old hand at the game. I carried it home and tied it in the cow yard, in the hope that if I planted myself out of sight the heifer might eventually pluck up enough resolution to pay it a visit. Nothing happened that day, so in the evening I was reduced to the necessity of trying to drive the heifer home. Something had to be done, because I couldn't leave her all night without milking her.

I mustered all my cows, drove them down on the heifer, collected her, and then headed them for the sheds.

Three times she broke away, and I patiently worked the cows back and got her again, and then finally, with the aid of a loud "Whoop!" and much noise, I shot her through the gate and got it closed on her. Although she was such a blood-thirsty creature, she didn't seem to have much heart when it came to fighting her own species, and while I was preparing things, my cows filled in time horning her around the yard.

I only had five cows in at the time, so I decided to milk them first, in case they got upset when I started to break in the heifer. I thought I might as well run the whole lot into the shed at once, and while I was busy with the cows, the heifer could have a look round and get used to things. The first thing she inspected in my shed was a gap under the door about six inches wide. She got down on her knees and tried to crawl through it, and when I hauled her back by the tail she doubled like an eel, and I escaped sudden death by half an inch. I let her out into the yard again so that I could milk the cows in peace, and then I nipped over to a neighbour, and asked him to come and help me. Sam Turner isn't the kind of man I would choose to help on a job like that, as a rule, but he lived close by, and it was a case of go for the nearest.

Sam has a squeaky voice, and is inclined to be excitable. He has great ideas about everything. Sam can sit by his fire in the evening, and explain how to break in the wildest outlaw, horse or heifer that ever lived. One great theory of his is to fix the animal to be subdued with a steely eye, and mesmerize it. When we got over to my place he had worked out a plan of battle, and as we entered the shed, he was telling me not to be afraid to call on him again in the morning if I had further trouble. Sam didn't anticipate I would, after he had settled her, but he said he could always spare a few minutes to help a friend. We got a rope and made a running noose on it for a start. I got up in front of a bail with one end, and Sam fixed his steely eye on the heifer, which was backed into a corner of the shed, lowering at us, with only the whites of its eyes showing.

My New Heifer

"When I slip the noose over her horns, you pull her up into the bail," said Sam, and advanced slowly. I hadn't much faith in Sam's idea myself, but I didn't like to hurt his feelings by telling him so. I thought he might be right, and anyway he couldn't do much harm trying it. When I went over to get Sam's help, I was under the impression I told him the heifer was wild. I thought he understood that was why I wanted his help. But after I had woodened the heifer with a sledge-hammer, and dragged Sam out on to the grass by his heels, he said, "No!" He said he wouldn't have dreamed of coming over if he had known she was like that. He wanted to know what he had ever done to me to warrant my putting such a dirty one across him, and when I wanted to help him to his feet he said I was to keep my murdering paws off him. I listened for a while, and then went away to get the Embrocation bottle, but I needn't have troubled. When I got back with it Sam had disappeared, and was halfway back home. I followed his track back by listening to the groans as he crossed fences and creeks, but I didn't know until later that he had done the whole distance on his hands and knees. After Sam had gone I began to ponder.

I went into the shed, and had a good look all round. There was a beam going right across the roof, about eight feet from the ground, so I climbed on to that, and tried lassooing the heifer from above. After several misses I managed to get it round her neck, and then I climbed quietly down with the end in my hand, and ran it through the front of one bail and back down another. Then I stood in the one bail, and hauled her up by the neck. It was a good job she was small, or I would never have handled her, but finally, by taking advantage of every time she rushed forward, I had her safely bailed up, and her head tied in as well. But the fun had only started. When I went to leg-rope her, I found she could balance herself on one leg and kick with the other three all at once.

After I had both hind legs tied, she fell down in such an attitude, that it was a case of let her go again or choke her.

Then I did it all over again with the same result. During quiet moments — when I was trying to undo a knot that had jammed before the rope broke her leg or strangled her — my mind dwelt lingeringly on the man who had sold her to me.

I hoped I would meet him again, so that I could express my gratitude in a fitting manner.

Every time the well-bred little thing let out a bellow, or went through a spasm of shuddery flinches, I saw that man's face, and heard his voice in my ear, advising me to hand feed her, and I would have her following me round like a dog. Before I could milk her I had to put two ropes across underneath her, to prevent her from going down. Then I got about a cup full of milk, and comforted myself with the reflection that she would probably give more in the morning. I went to the factory next morning before I attempted to milk her, and after going through exactly the same procedure as the night before, I got another cup of milk. I did this for a week, and neither she nor I got used to it. So finally I turned the calf on to her and shut her away in my back paddock.

Then I waded in and did all the work I had neglected while I was subduing her, and went out the back to see how she was getting on, just in time to save the calf's life. That well-bred little thing wasn't producing enough milk to nourish her own calf, and the poor little beggar was simply fading away. I had to bring it home and bucket feed it again, and then I hunted around and tried to find someone I could give that heifer to.

Several people accepted her, but none of them ever got her past the middle paddock of my farm, so in the end I went back there with a gun.

* * * * * * * *

That was the year something went wrong with the hide market, and when I took the skin into town it fetched one and sixpence.

* * * * * * * *

My New Heifer

The only sort of heifer I buy now is the sort you can go up to and pet in the paddock.

Helping Out Gus

I'm not what you'd call a ladies' man at all. Far from it! I'm the sort of fellow you often see in the back blocks. I take a girl four or five miles to a hop, and sit in a corner half the night, twiddling my watch chain, or tearing pieces of paper into small bits, while she does the supper dance, every other, and the last, with some good-looking stranger from the city.

Then I drive her home, and she goes into raptures all the way back, talking about the nice boy she met — "Didn't I notice him?" Then, when I say I didn't, and ask who the queer-looking chap was she had the supper waltz with, there's a row.

That's me! I have a friend though, who isn't quite such a dismal failure as I am. He loses his head over a fresh girl about every three or four months. He likes to have me about with him he says, to act as a foil. I don't know if I quite liked that, I wanted to know how. Then he explained, him being broad and fair, and me thin, bony and sallow, it sort of set him off.

It sort of set me off too, and it took him a minute or two to explain what he really did mean. He said, "You know Mark, you tough wiry chaps are all a bit hot-tempered, that's why the girls all go nap on you the way they do." I hadn't noticed it, but I took a swig at the drink he pushed at me, and decided that perhaps I wasn't very observant. I decided to keep my eyes open next girl I talked to. I have an idea I could get on much better with girls if I didn't have any hands or feet, hands especially. It doesn't matter what I do with my hands, they don't seem to be in the right place. Now there's the difference between old Gus Tomlins and me. He's the friend I'm telling you about. Gus can stand in the midst of a bevy of topping looking girls and smile, chat and look as natural, as detached and nonchalant as a dog on the hearth rug.

I always knew when Gus was going through the mill. He has a wheezy old motorcycle and side-car, and when little Cupid is playing a joke on him, you can hear this affair backfiring and roaring over at Gus's place at all hours of the day and night.

Helping Out Gus

I live next to Gus, and he can't slip out without me knowing about it. That cycle makes such a noise climbing the hill next to me that it wakes every neighbour for half a mile round when he is coming home. Now and then, say one week in every quarter, Gus decides to cut out all this silly love stuff, and comes over to my place and interrupts me at my work.

He sits about, looking dreary and solemn, and passes strange remarks about the rotten world, and what a miserable, small, shallow lot of people live in it, until I get fidgety and uncomfortable myself. Then he switches off that, and starts to give me a lot about sticking to his friends. He always does. He goes on to explain just how much he thinks of me, and how he has found out at last, that a true-blue friend like myself is worth all the girls in the country. I know what's coming after that. Gus hasn't got a lady friend just for the time, and sooner than go by himself, he wants me to ride in his side-car with him to the next dance.

And I'm always mug enough to accept the offer. Last year we went ten miles to a fancy dress ball. I was done up as a ballet girl, and when Gus arrived with his buzzer at my gate, I just slipped on an overcoat over the rig-out, and stepped into the side-car. I had my dancing pumps on as well. There didn't seem any need for boots, going right to the door of the dancing hall as we were. Gus was a bold hussar, and looked real good. The hop had started when we got inside, so we took a seat and piped off all the good-lookers. I could see Gus's eye following a tall, willowy fairy, as she waltzed round on the arm of a gentleman dressed as a devil. He was a big, husky fellow too. As soon as the dance was over, Gus hustled round, and got the next dance with her. I kept my eye on them because I always like to see old Gus interested in someone; it prevents him coming over about four nights a week, and sighing into my fire till after midnight.

They seemed to be hitting it pretty well together, and after the dance Gus came along to me.

He seemed clean off his head. He got me in a corner and said: "Now Mark, I rely on you. Don't fail me old man." Then he laid down his plan of campaign. He was to take me along, and give me an introduction to her. We were to try to wangle things so that we should have every other dance with her, and sit one on each side as well. I had to tell her, in a make conversation sort of way, what a great pal old Gus was, and slip in a few allusions about his big house, his pedigree herd, and how well he was doing. I didn't mind. There was no one at the dance I could work up any enthusiasm over, and I thought I might just as well be boosting old Gus along as filling in time any other way. There was no danger of me losing my head over her. The tall, dignified ones don't appeal to me. I like short, plump girls, with soft, round faces. After I had my instructions, Gus ambled me over to the fairy, and introduced us. "Mr. Turner, Miss O'Flynn." I booked the next dance. Then we sat one on each side of her, as arranged, and Gus got in for the next, just in time to beat the gentleman done up as Old Nick. Nick hovered about in front of us for a while, giving me a particularly baneful glare, as if he expected to bluff me out of my position next to the fairy. I replied by modestly pulling my ballet dress as far over my knees, as it would go, and peeping coyly at him from behind my fan.

He made a noise like a cat sneezing and headed for the door. "What a rough, uncouth fellow!" said Gus, in a pained tone.

The fairy didn't say anything, she only giggled, and I must say I draw the line at a giggling girl. Gus doesn't however, all the girls he gets in tow with are the giggling kind.

She went up one with him straight away. Nick didn't show up any more, and Gus and I whacked up the next four or five dances between us. Anyone else who toddled along to try his luck got left out. Then I thought I had done enough of this hold the fort stunt, even if Gus was a mate of mine, and I slipped out into the porch for a smoke. I was just holding the match to my pipe to light up when a hand about as big as a leg of mutton grasped me by the lace frill round my neck. I dropped pipe and match to gaze into the sulphurous eyes of Satan himself.

"Look out, you'll tear my clothes!"

"If you go back and sit by that girl again, I'll tear the heart out of you," said Satan in a cold, nasty voice.

"Little squib like you! What ya' mean by it?"

I saw this was a case for tact. No good me getting into a mix up over a girl I didn't even admire. I sympathized with Nick, really. I've been there myself, so I answered mildly, "All right old chap, I won't."

He let me go then, after waggling his fist up and down past my off ear, just to show me what a savage person he was, and I managed to sneak into the hall again. There was no need for me to go back and sit by the fairy anyhow. She had forgotten I ever existed, and she and Gus were doing every dance together.

That's where Gus and I differ. I never could stick this every dance together stuff. Just to see anyone doing it gives me a kind of sick, creepy feeling. After each dance, he would hold her hand and tell fortunes. I knew he was doing that, because once he read up an article on hand reading, in some magazine, and he works his knowledge off on every girl who is fool enough to lend him her hand. I didn't go near him again, but I could spot from right across the room just what was happening. The marriage line made her giggle, and the life line pulled her up with a jerk; it must have had a break or two in it I expect. Nick kept on peeping through the door, but they didn't take the slightest notice of him. I felt sorry for that chap. I remembered having a somewhat similar experience once, myself.

Lots of people think it's funny to see a chap dippy over a girl, but my personal experience is that's how murders, and such like, occur.

I felt a mild curiosity to see how Gus would get on after the hop was over. I had an idea he was going to have a thrilling experience once he got outside the hall, and the big chap got hold of him. I put a bob in each trouser pocket and bet myself a shilling Nick knocked him out inside of three hits. Then after supper, I got a bit interested in a flappy little girl who worked in a lolly shop, and wished she lived on a farm, because she simply loved animals, and all that rot, and I forgot to keep an eye on Gus for a time. The next thing I knew, I heard a noise like a one-inch pom-pom tearing off a thousand rounds, and I rushed outside just in time to see the motorbike and side-car turning a corner, with two people aboard.

I guessed straight away. They had watched their chance to dodge Nick, and then slipped quietly out and made their getaway. Gus was taking her home. I call that a low-down trick myself, taking another chap's girl home, but Gus always quotes Shakespeare, or whoever it is, when I tell him that, and says, "All's fair in love and war."

Nick arrived on the scene while I was still gazing into the black night, listening to that rattle-trap old engine. He seemed to blame me, and I had a lot of trouble explaining just whereabouts in the picture I really did fit. I got him calmed down at last, and went inside to fill in time till Gus got back to take me home. I gave him half an hour, because the fairy had told both of us early in the evening that she lived six miles away. Nick had driven her to the dance in his gig. The half an hour went by, the last dance came to an end, but still no Gus!

I glanced at my watch. Three in the morning, ten miles from home, and I had a herd of cows at home with nobody to milk them but me. Worse still, I had left my overcoat rolled up in the side-car, and Gus had taken it with him, and all I had for footwear was a pair of very light pumps. I knew what had happened. That ramshackle old Noah's Ark of Gus's had exploded, or run into a motor lorry, and it was no use looking for Gus to turn up. I decided I should have to walk. I tore the lace frills off and tied my pumps on my feet with them, and then I made a start.

I shall never forget that journey. Every dog that lived in that ten-mile strip came out and chased me past the particular farm he lived on. I suppose I did look a bit of a suspicious character. I wasn't half way when the sun started to rise, and I could hear people all round getting in their cows. I hoped they'd be too busy to spot me, but my luck was out. An old chap named Haggenbach — I have an idea he was of foreign origin — was driving his cows across the road just as I got to his place. Those cows took one startled look at me, and went off down the road at a gallop. I suppose the sight of a ballet dress at 4:30 a.m. is a bit unusual, but I fail to see that it should raise the excitement it did.

Old Haggenbach took one furious glance at me and then opened out.

"Mine Yimminy! You fright mine cow, you teifil! I keel you."

Then he ran to a seven wire fence and tore a batten off it with a single jerk. It's a good job I met Haggenbach that morning, because I would never have got my cows milked in time to catch the factory if it hadn't been for him. I gained nearly half an hour there I bet. I got home at last. However, just as I was letting myself in the front gate, Gus roared past at about 25 miles an hour. I knew he was making that because the old bus was clanging and shrieking like a harbour dredge in action, and that's always a sign that she's fully extended. Gus came over that night to tell me what had happened. I received him coldly, but listened in silence. I have an idea that perhaps Gus could clean me up if we ever mixed things, and it's no use looking for trouble when that's how you feel. Gus says he got within two miles of the girl's home and then had a puncture. When he went to look for his "mendif" outfit, or "stickfase," or whatever they call it; he couldn't find it. He messed about with his pump trying to pump up a tube with an inch split in it, afraid to tell the girl the worst, and while he was jigging away, along came Nick himself in his gig. Nick pulled up and the fairy just clambered out of the side-car and into the gig without a word. Then Nick pushed the reins into her hands and said, "Hold the reins Mary, while I get out and wipe the dirt with that snipe." Then Mary clung to him and said, "No, Will dear, he isn't worth it." That's the part that hurts, says Gus.

Personally, if it had been my funeral, that would be the only part of it I wouldn't mind dwelling on, because Will allowed himself to be calmed down and didn't get out.

They passed a few cheap remarks to Gus and then drove off and left him. Gus says it's a good job he didn't get out, because if he had, someone would have got hurt. I think so myself.

Mark and Gus

As soon as the road was clear of them Gus dived into the side-car and found his outfit first hit. She must have been sitting on it all the time, and he hadn't brains enough to ask her to stand up while he searched.

He had three more punctures on the homeward journey, that's why I beat him to my gate, and he reckons some of his bonus will have to go towards new tyres and tubes one of these days. I asked him what he thought when he got back to the hall and found I wasn't there.

He gave a start and said, "You don't suppose I had time to think of you, do you, with all the troubles I was having?"

I don't like that sort of talk myself, it sounds selfish. He went on to say that a man who was really a friend wouldn't think tuppence of a little walk like that when it couldn't be helped.

When he went on, and blamed me for the whole business; we had words. He said if it hadn't been for me egging him on and putting the idea into his head, he would never have thought of taking the girl home. We parted real snarky at the finish, and Gus wouldn't look my side of the road for a week. Then one evening he breezed into the bach as large as life and said, "Mark old man, do us a favour, will you?"

So, like a mug again, I said, "Yes, what is it?" and Gus proceeded to unbosom himself. It was a girl who was a waitress in a tea shop in town, and all he wanted me to do was to go into town with him in the jigger, and drop in there casually by myself and ask if Mr. Tomlins had been in.

When she asked who Mr. Tomlins was, I was to say, "What? Don't know Mr. Tomlins? Why, Mr. Tomlins, the great Jersey cattle man, of course."

Now, that's the sort of thing old Gus puts across me, and the worst of it is, I'm too good-natured to refuse.

See the idea? While I'm explaining who Mr. Tomlins is, Gus walks in himself, and of course that's when I introduce him, and then fade out of the picture.

Some fellow, Gus is!

Gus Buys a Horse

Gus Tomlins is a mate of mine. Every time he gets into difficulties, he comes over to my place and wants me to help him out. Of course I don't mind, and, as a matter of fact, it's rather interesting. Only I do hate this rotten style some people have of taking all the credit if they pull off some fancy stunt, and trying to shuffle out of all the blame if things go wrong. Now there was the time Gus wanted to buy a horse to do his autumn ploughing. He asked me to go with him to the horse-mart; said my opinion would count a good deal, because everyone knew what a good judge of horses I was. I went with him, and he fixed his eye on a big chestnut gelding with a wall-eye and puffy legs. Said that was his idea of a horse. It was no use my pointing out that the animal looked bad-tempered, and wasn't built for heavy work. No! Gus reckoned he'd be just the animal for a bit of ploughing, and probably his puffy legs were due to the fact that he was a bit of a sprinter. Trotting on hard roads always puffed a horse's legs up. Presently the horse was put up for auction.

The owner led him round the ring. Guaranteed sound in wind and limb; quiet; go anywhere, do anything; pedigree a yard long.

"Can he plough?" chipped in Gus.

Oh yes, he could plough. The owner had used him to plough twenty acres, and then lent him to all the neighbours to do their ploughing.

So Gus bought him for £18, and got me to lead him home, because he had to take the motorcycle back.

When I got him out to Gus's farm, Gus had a feed of chaff ready, and an old cover he had dug up from somewhere. He said he thought he had a bargain if he looked after it, and probably he'd get about forty pounds for him next spring. He said he would call him Ginger, because anyone could see the horse was high-spirited.

Then he gave the horse the feed, and got kicked while he was doing up the back straps of the cover.

He had to pay a man to come and run his farm for a fortnight while his leg got right. He used to fill in the evenings explaining to sympathetic visitors that the horse was all right, only he didn't suppose the poor beast had ever had a cover on in its life before. When his leg got better he would show us just how to handle that sort of nervous animal. It only wanted kindness and plenty of quiet confidence.

Soon after Gus's leg got well enough to enable him to get about again, he called on me. "I'll be using Ginger to plough the paddock tomorrow Mark; better come over and watch him work. Then you might be satisfied he's all right." I didn't promise, and Gus left under the impression that I wouldn't come over because I was too stiff-necked to eat my own words. He said he couldn't understand a man who wouldn't give in when everything proved him wrong.

After I'd cleaned up everything next morning, I was standing on the milk-can stand enjoying a quiet smoke, when I fancied I heard shouting and yelling over at the back of Gus's. "Hullo! Gus got kicked again," I thought, and rushed off across.

When I arrived I found Gus and his team having high old jinks. His other old horse, Darky, was standing at ease, looking bored to death, while Ginger was sitting on the mould-board of the plough, with his eyes shut and his ears back. Gus's idea about just how to handle that sort of nervous beast was in full swing, and consisted of kicking him until he got tired, and then punching him until he put his thumb out. He quietened down sufficiently after a time to get his voice back, and then asked me in a trembly tone to go and get his gun.

Of course, that's all rot. As I pointed out to him, what's the use of shooting a good moke like that, just because he's high-spirited? From what I could gather, Ginger just simply refused to budge, and when Gus got wild and went to his head to demand an explanation, he backed until he hit the plough, and then just sat on it.

Gus Buys a Horse

I rather fancy myself about how to handle horses, so I said I would have a go. I took the collar and chains off Ginger, and then asked him to stand up. He did so, as meekly as a lamb, so then I said, "Collar proud!" in a satisfied voice, as if I had thought so all along, and told Gus to go and get a set of light chain harrows, and we would try him on his own. We put him in the harrows, and he went round the paddock with them as quiet and well-behaved as you could wish. As I kept explaining to Gus, all a man wants when he's handling these high-spirited beasts is plenty of patience and self-confidence, and if he only treats them with kindness and understanding he must win out.

At dinner time Gus went away to get Darky, and I was supposed to drive Ginger home with the harrows. We had decided not to try and plough that day, but to give Ginger plenty of chain-harrow drill, and stick him in the plough in the morning.

I will say this for Gus. He gave me all the credit, and kept saying, "Mark, I don't know what I should have done without you. I might have ruined a good horse. Look at him; quiet and steady as any horse in the district."

Then he dodged off to get Darky, and I went ahead to open the gate, and before I could pick up the reins again, Ginger had bolted through it, and was off at a gallop, harrows and all. We watched him until he tried to take the eight-foot harrows through a three-foot wicket gate near the house, and then we broke into a run.

We arrived just as Ginger kicked himself clear.

Gus said the horse was an out-and-out jibber, but a horse that can pull out two gate posts, and then break a trace chain and his hames strap, is no jibber.

Ginger stood in the yard the remainder of the day, and kicked out at everything which crossed an imaginary circle he had mapped out, about thirty feet across. No wonder he had puffy legs. We left him alone, and Gus said that as I had got him into this mess, I had better come with him tomorrow and help him out of it.

Mark and Gus

About eleven o'clock next morning Gus and I started off in the motorcycle and side-car. We paid a visit to the auctioneering firm the horse was sold by, and found out the address of the previous owner. Then we called on him. He was a shifty-eyed man of about fifty, and was surprised to see us:

"Horse wouldn't plough! That's funny! Sure you treated him right?"

Gus said he had.

"Hmm! Well, if you bring him out here, I'll stick him in and give you a trial. Will that satisfy you?"

Gus thought it would.

The farmer went on to state that he had ploughed miles with that horse, he had, and it seemed a mighty queer thing to him that people should keep him for over a fortnight, and then complain that he was no good. As usual, he directed his remarks at me. I can't understand how it is, if Gus and I are together, and anyone doesn't like us, they always talk at me.

Then when we get away by ourselves Gus will say, "Mark, I wonder how you stuck that. If anyone had spoken to me like that I'd have cracked them."

Then if I get huffy, he says I'm a queer bloke, and a man daren't speak to me for fear of offending me.

I expect I shall end up having a row with Gus one of these days.

I had to waste another day on that horse.

Gus wanted me to ride and lead Ginger out there to the farmer while he rode the motorbike out, but I drew the line there. I said if it was too much trouble for him to lead his own horse, it was too much trouble for me to go at all.

We finally decided to drive out in my gig, and lead Ginger. All the way out Gus kept grumbling about what a rickety turn-out it was, and promising me to let me down the very first time I came over to him to ask him a favour. When we got out to the farmer's, he wasn't at home, so we tied the horse up and waited an hour. Then we decided to leave Ginger and drive home without the trial he was going to give us. We had just got nicely settled in the gig, and were going out of the gate, when Gus turned round for a last fond look at Ginger, and spotted the farmer peeping over a hedge about ten yards away.

So then we got out again and surrounded him. He said he couldn't give us a trial that day because he didn't happen to have a paddock that wanted ploughing. He suggested we take the horse away and come back, say in a month.

Gus wanted him to put the horse in, and just plough one furrow round a calf paddock near his house. I never heard a man make such a fuss as that farmer did.

What! Plough up a good grass paddock just because we didn't know how to handle a good horse? He'd see us further, he would. He ended his remarks by alluding to me as a cross-eyed spieler, and said he could see by my looks that I just lived by sucking the life-blood out of honest farmers.

I got pretty wild at that. I told him straight that if he didn't mind himself, I'd inform the police. Then we drove away and left Ginger tied up at his old home.

About half a mile down the road a fellow stopped us, and wanted to know why we had brought old Spinner's horse back. He told us that the horse was a rank outlaw, and that before Spinner could get him quiet enough to take him into the sale-yards, he had paid a horse-breaker three pounds ten to educate him enough to lead, and accept the bit in his mouth without trying for a few fingers as well.

Gus had to send old Spinner a lawyer's letter before he got his eighteen pounds back, and a week or so after that, someone saw Spinner in the horse-mart selling a big chestnut gelding: "Quiet, steady, reliable. Go anywhere, do anything."

He got fifteen pounds for him that time and all I hope is that the poor beggar that bought him didn't get killed before he had time to repent of his bargain.

I never allude to Ginger when Gus is about, because somehow or other Gus has got the idea into his head that I bought the horse for him, or persuaded him against his better judgement to take him, and the way he harps on about how smart he was getting clear of a bad bargain, it fairly makes my flesh creep. If

I hadn't come messing round Gus reckons, he believes he could have cured that horse of jibbing and kicking, but of course I had to come poking my nose into it and spoil everything.

He borrows my horse to do his ploughing with now, because as he explains, I probably lost him twenty pounds when I let old Ginger clear out. Everybody knows a horse is goosed after it has cleared out once, and twenty pounds would have bought two old crocks like the one I lend him.

It was a bit of a jar to hear him talk like that because every time I tot up my available assets I always head the list with "One horse, £50."

But that's just like Gus. He's going to get a surprise some of these days when he comes over for a horse and I tell him I am going to use the horse myself.

Wood-Splitting with Gus

The year of the great butter slump, when all the cow farmers were doing a starve, Gus Tomlins came to me one day with a brilliant suggestion.

His idea was that he and I should get the firewood rights on a thousand acre section, up under the mountain reserve. He said we could hop in that winter while the cows were dry, and knock up anything up to a fiver a day each. It sounded pretty good to me. Even allowing for a bit of exaggeration on Gus's part — he's inclined that way — I could see myself doing pretty well at it; say two pounds to two pounds ten a day. Of course, as I pointed out to Gus, what did he know about firewood splitting anyhow? But he seemed to think I would be the drawback.

Gus says that all you have to do splitting wood is to keep your eye on the grain, and not get your wedges stuck in any knots. It's the simplest game out according to Gus. Plenty of muscle and grit, and a man can knock up a cord to two cord a day if he strikes decent timber. We bustled round that winter and got permission to cut wood on the section; the owner charging us two shillings a cord royalty. Then we collected a cross-cut saw, five or six wedges, an axe, and a sledge-hammer, and settled to our work. We sold our wood for fifteen shillings a cord at the stump, and that gave us thirteen bob a cord for ourselves after paying the royalty. It didn't seem such a wonderful snip to me, after I had worked it out on paper.

Even supposing we knocked up two cord a day each, which I was inclined to doubt, it only gave us twenty-six bob for a day's graft, and when a man has listened to Gus talking fivers for weeks, twenty-six bob doesn't seem much. I don't mind admitting that times were hard, or Gus would never have lured me into any such foolishness. That's the real reason I never got married long ago. Just to think of the amount of firewood the average woman wants chopped every day gives me a sad, sick feeling. All I have to do now is pull a batten off a fence, and that boils my kettle three times.

When a man has such decided ideas on wood-splitting as that, you can easy imagine how hard up I was to tackle knocking up cord wood.

The first day we started on the job we had a lot of trouble with the saw. We could set it to saw down about six inches and then it used to jam. Gus knew what was wrong though. He said it was want of set, and asked me to pass him the sledge-hammer and a wedge. Gus said it was a funny thing, he had often noticed it, how some men went through life, year after year, and never learnt a single useful thing. Take setting a saw, for instance! He said he didn't suppose I could set a saw even if I had a saw-set to do it with, and the best thing I could do now was watch him, in case I ever had to do it myself.

Then he laid the saw along the log, slipped the wedge under every other tooth, and tapped each one with the sledgehammer. He broke off three, but that didn't matter. It helped the saw to clear itself, he reckoned. Then we started again, and made a gash in the log about half an inch wide.

We had no more bother with the saw jamming, but after we got down about a foot it seemed to want to turn round and saw its way up again. Gus said it was running a shade, but that was nothing, we could counteract that by changing the saw end for end every now and again. We changed the saw like that about four times in a four-foot log, and when we finally got through we could have used the block for a step-ladder.

There were two old chaps over the fence from us who were splitting wood as well, and Gus and I decided it would be interesting to see how much more we split every day than they did. We didn't try to break any records the first day. For one thing we lost nearly ten minutes while Gus set the saw, and I always reckon myself that if you are out to get a big day in, the start is the most important part. I sawed off the next block myself while Gus swung the sledge-hammer. About every third blow the head would fly off it, and just because it was my hammer Gus got sarcastic about it.

Wood-Splitting with Gus

He said he went to the trouble of supplying the gang with a decent saw, and setting it, and I couldn't even be trusted to bring along a sledge-hammer that a man could use. I pointed out that I had seen that old saw stopping a gap in his barberry hedge for about three years, and how long it was there before that, goodness only knows. It's no use arguing with Gus when he feels put out, it only makes him worse. He said the saw was two! Up to get seasoned, any fool should know that much.

We wasted a good bit of time thrashing the matter out, and the sun seemed to set on us before we really knew the day had started. The miserable little heap of cord we had split wasn't worth stacking up, and we made up our minds to do considerably better next day. The first day on these sort of jobs is always heart-breaking, Gus and I both agreed to that, but, of course, after we had got used to the tools and our muscles set to the work, we would begin to make things fly.

Next morning we arrived on the scene bright and early.

"We'll dig in hard Mark, and show those two old jokers over the fence how to smack up wood," remarked old Gus. He had dug up an old running singlet from somewhere, one of those chain-net affairs without any sleeves, and was standing at the heap of wood doubling his arms and admiring his muscles. I got filled with enthusiasm myself just looking at him, and tore off my shirt and flannel so that I would not be behind him in hardiness. Next minute we were at it like a pair of frenzied lunatics. Every time I wanted a spell from the saw I used to double round and grab the sledge-hammer from Gus, and he would nip back and do some sawing. When there was no more wood to split, both of us would saw. We gobbled our lunches down in ten minutes, didn't wait for a smoke even, and buckled into it again. Once, as I straightened my aching back for a moment, I glanced over the fence and noticed the two old chaps over there. They were both sitting on their log looking our way, and puffing up clouds of tobacco smoke. It gave me new life only to see them wasting precious moments like that.

By five o'clock we were dead beat, but we had a pile of wood that filled us with pride.

Mark and Gus

Gus estimated it to be between three and four cord, and tired as we were, we decided to stack it up before going home. We had slung it on top of the wood split the first day, and when we got the lot stacked we got a slight surprise, because measure as carefully as we could, it wouldn't pan out more than one and a quarter cords. Well, I did some mental arithmetic going home, and told Gus to count me out of his wood-splitting gang because I had an idea I was sickening from lumbago. I was so stiff and sore for the next three days that I couldn't have worked on the job, even if I hadn't retired, and I knew Gus was feeling the same. What hurt most of all was the fact that those two old chaps over the fence had knocked up over two cord that day, and I know myself they had an hour off for lunch time, and two quarters of an hour 'smoke-ohs'. Gus didn't seem too keen on wood-splitting himself for over a week, and then he dropped in on me one evening and started to upbraid me for being a quitter. I can be pretty firm when I like, and I told him straight out that I was done with wood-splitting and it was no use; he might just as well talk to himself as talk wood to me.

He kept on arguing that way, and finally came to light with a suggestion which sounded a good deal more sensible than anything he had thought of previously. He said: "Look here Mark, if I get old Harry Pope, the wood-splitter, to join us, will you make one then?" We chewed that over for some time. Old Harry is an old chap about eighty, who has done nothing but split wood all his life.

Everybody in the district knows him, and he has a great reputation.

One of these cord-a-day men, any timber, all weathers. Gus's idea was that we give Harry two bob an hour for himself and tools — he admitted our tools weren't up to much — and anything old Harry made over his wages everyday would be ours. That appealed to me; I always did like making money that way, and so I came into the gang again.

Old Harry was a little old chap with watery eyes, and a white whisker all round his face. He used to chew a two ounce plug of tobacco up every day, and didn't seem to care much where he spat. We got back on the job again on a frosty Monday morning, and Harry upset us a good deal by taking two hours to sharpen his saw. While he was doing that Gus formulated some rules for the gang. Harry and I were to saw, and as he was the only man in the gang who knew how to swing a sledge-hammer — that's what he said — he would do all the splitting. As soon as the old chap had fixed up the saw, we tried it out on a big rata log, about five feet through. Gus sat alongside, explaining to me why I would never be any good at the game. According to him I did everything wrong; he said no wonder he and I couldn't make the game pay, if that's how I stood and pulled on my end. He could see watching me, that it wasn't his good saw that was to blame after all, and if he had only noticed what a rotten sawer I was, before he had engaged old Harry, he could have done without him, and saved sixteen bob a day.

He didn't bother to get the other old relic and start on another log although I pointed out that, as he was so good, that would be the way to show us, but said he expected he would have enough to do before the day was out, splitting for the two of us.

I don't like wearing a hat when I am working, but I found out it was just as well to have it on when sawing wood with old Harry. He's been splitting and sawing firewood on his own for so many years that he's got into the habit of just tilting his head and squirting his 'bacca juice over the log he is working at. It saves him turning his neck, I suppose. I didn't have a hat on the first time it happened, and I walked round the log to see him about it. Gus said I was a darn poor sport; any fool could see it was an accident, and anyhow, why should I cut up rough over a little thing like that. If I was going to be so contrary and quarrelsome, he could see us not making a pound a day even. I went back to my end of the saw as soon as I knew old Harry hadn't done it on purpose, and we sawed away in savage silence until we had a length off. Then Gus got the hammer and wedges and started off to keep us busy. Harry caught me in the ear with his second chew, almost as soon as we had started the next log, and I nearly broke up the partnership. After that I took to wearing my hat, and keeping a handkerchief tied round my neck. I never really got used to it, but I learned to saw away and suffer in silence. That day we did some good cross-cut work, and we certainly kept Gus going.

By three in the afternoon we had four cuts off the log, and Gus was still banging and swearing over the first. Then he slung his hammer down and started to go off about people who came into a partnership and picked out all the easiest work. I left the saw and went and had a look. He had all our six wedges hammered into a twisty, stringy piece of wood, and it hadn't started to split even. I asked him why he hadn't followed the grain instead of fooling about in that silly fashion, and he replied so earnestly that his voice cracked, and made old Harry swallow his chew. Then the two old chaps over the fence came running across, under the impression one of us had got hurt, and they had a look at things. They said it was a black mountain rata, and about the worst kind of rata there is to split. They wouldn't dream of tackling one themselves, and why hadn't we tried the first cut before we sawed the whole tree up?

Personally, they wouldn't split those blocks up for pounds. We didn't split them up either. As soon as they had gone I went and put my coat on, and when I got back I found Gus trying to explain to old Harry that he was sacked, and telling him he could have the wedges in the log if he liked to get them out.

We left old Harry collecting tools and mumbling to himself, and Gus and I each took a different track back home. I never found out who got the money for the cord and a quarter we had split. Gus and I never, anyhow. We forked out eight bob each to old Harry, and as far as I'm concerned, I reckon I had a cheap let off. No more wood-splitting for me. Give me a good honest old milking stool and a shed full of cows. Every time I think of Gus and I tearing into that wood and knocking up a cord and a quarter in two hectic days, I get a faint, sick feeling.

Our Quiet Winter

The winter before last Gus came over to my bach one day with one of his brilliant ideas. He said it was silly he and I running two separate establishments all the winter. Why not club together and live in one show? We could share the tucker bill, and it would make things easier all round. I wasn't keen on the idea at all. I like old Gus so long as I don't see him too often, but I didn't have any say in it, as it happened.

Gus just decided it was a real brainy idea, and shifted his bedding across that night. He chose my bach for us to live in because I had got my winter supply of firewood snigged home, whereas Gus had been too busy to waste time on a luxury like firewood.

He started to find fault with things straight away. After tea, the first thing that took his eye was the dog licking out the frying pan. I can't see any harm in that myself, but Gus said it was sickening, and started to roll his eyes and to try to remember if I'd washed it out before I fried the sausages. As I pointed out to him, there's generally a cat sleeping in his frying pan any time I drop in to see him. I knew how it was going to be — as soon as Gus got settled down in my shack he was going to start picking things to pieces. He said a cat was a domesticated animal, it was allowed inside, but dogs were different. I always let my dog sit by the fire with me of an evening; he's good company, and another thing, if a man keeps his dog inside he knows where he is. That didn't suit Gus at all. I had to keep the dog outside. Gus rolled his bedding out on the floor the first night. He promised himself a bush stretcher as soon as he had time to knock one together, but in the meantime the floor would do. He kept tossing and growling half the night, and calling it dog-fleas, just to make me feel uncomfortable. About 2 a.m. he let out a roar, and I nearly jumped out of my old shake-down with fright. I sat up and looked over at Gus's corner.

He was swearing and wiping the heads off matches, so I lit a candle to see what was wrong. Gus swore that an animal as big as a sheep dog had stepped on his face. I told him he had eaten too many pork sausages it was a nightmare he had.

"No," said Gus, "it wasn't a nightmare, because I haven't had a wink of sleep yet." Then I remembered that Gus's bed was placed close to the wall that had a rat hole in it. Every night two or three of them used to pay me a visit, and clean up all the crumbs on the table. They didn't know about Gus, and I suppose one of them had hopped through the hole on to his face. Gus made as much fuss over it as if they were fancy-trained rats and I had done it on purpose. He stood in the middle of the room mumbling to himself, and first running his palms down the calf of one leg and then the other, as if he were wiping them down. This time he called it rat-fleas, and got hasty when I said it was imagination. After a while he dragged his bedding along the floor a bit and turned in again. About 5 a.m. I got disturbed once more.

It was raining in torrents. I could hear it battering down on the roof by the bucketful, but that didn't seem sufficient reason for Gus to make such a rotten fuss. He was at it again with the matches too. I could see him painting streaks of phosphorus up and down the flooring, so I lit the candle once more. Then I knew what the trouble was. When Gus had shifted his bed during the night he had dragged it under the hole in the roof. I had been going to fix that leak for months, but Gus seemed to think I had climbed up there while he was asleep and punched a hole in the roof iron just for his benefit. He kept on harping about how the place was so draughty, and one thing and another, that he hadn't slept a solitary wink all night. I had to point out, in the finish, that it was a mighty funny thing how his bed had got so soaked with water if he had been lying there awake all the time. The first drop would have shifted me if I'd been under that leak, but Gus must have allowed the bed to soak up two or three gallons before he decided to stir. He went shivering out into the back porch for an old chaff-bag and a cow-cover I had there, and I lent him one of my blankets for the rest of the morning. At breakfast time he stretched strings all across the kitchen, and had his blankets hanging everywhere. I didn't mind having to bob and duck every time I wanted to get near the fire, but I drew the line at seeing a wet blanket dripping on to the butter and sugar while we were eating. Gus said I was a queer chap. He supposed I wanted him to lay the seeds of rheumatics and neuralgia by sleeping in wet blankets! Then I had to speak plainly. I said I didn't mind him living in the place, only why couldn't he act reasonable? He'd spoilt my night's rest for me, growling and grunting over little things all night long, and now he was trying to turn the show into a steam laundry.

Then Gus got wild and tore all the blankets down and heaved them into a corner. After breakfast he went away to feed out hay to his cows, and I went off to look after mine. I got back first and stoked up the fire and hung all the bedding up again.

It teemed down steadily all that day, and after Gus had built a sack stretcher to sleep on and had plugged up the rat hole in the wall, we sat about, in a sour, yellow looking steam, and kept ourselves amused shifting the blankets about as they dried.

It rained without ceasing for four miserable days, and Gus and I put in the time squabbling over who'd fry the steak and who'd peel the spuds. Things got so bad the fifth day that we both sat in front of the fire waiting for one another to go out and chop some wood until it gave a last flicker and went out. Then Gus stood up and stretched himself. "Look here Mark, I'm absolutely fed up with this," he said. "A man ought to have his head read anyhow, for being here at all." He glanced disdainfully around my habitation, and I sat up and snapped, "Who asked you to be here anyhow?" "Don't get snarky," said Gus. "Let's get out and have a change."

The idea appealed to me as soon as he mentioned it, so I said, "What about dropping along to the Treadwells, and challenging the girls to a game of coon-can?" Good enough! declared Gus; so we slipped into our oilskins and heavy boots and set off.

Mark and Gus

Mary Treadwell was out in the rain chopping stove wood when we arrived, and Gus gallantly took the axe away from her and smacked up an armful. That's Gus all over. He couldn't miss a chance to impress a girl, but he could sit by my fire and watch it go out without wanting to chop any. We found old Mr. Treadwell sitting over a big back-log in the front room. He had another old chap named Mr. Ginger with him. Gus and I didn't get a chance to challenge the girls. They were all out in the kitchen with their mother, and as soon as Mr. Treadwell saw us he exclaimed gleefully, "Aha! Just the two men we want. Sit up here, and Mr. Ginger and I will teach you how to play crib." I know how to play crib, only I don't like the game. The counting always makes me get spots before the eyes, but Gus jumped at the suggestion, so I had to take a hand. "The two good players will play against the two poor," decided old Tready. "And that will show you two young fellows how experience tells in a game of cribbage." The first time round the board the two old chaps took turns at stopping me every time I led a card and explaining why it was I had no business to play that particular one. Gus rather fancies himself at crib, so they left him alone and directed all their benevolent advice to me. Gus and I won the first game by one hole, and the old boys put their pipes down and started to play. They had a lot of cheery remarks to pass about "beginners' luck", and "giving us the first game to hearten us up," and that sort of talk, but I noticed I didn't get any more fatherly advice on how to play my hand. I started off in the second game by holding two lots of 18 each and 16 in crib. We won that game before they had gone once round the board, and old Ginger commenced getting offensive. He said it was impossible to play crib against a man who violated every rule of the game the way I did. In the third game Gus stopped old Tready from taking Ginger's hand twice on the pegs, and after we had won it Tready got up and stamped outside. We heard him loosing three hungry dogs, and after he had dogged the pigs away from the verandah he came in and started again.

Our Quiet Winter

On the fourth game the old chaps got a good lead on us and about half way through Mrs. Treadwell came into the room with a tray full of cups of tea.

"Take that stuff away," roared Mr. Treadwell. "Can't you see we're busy?" Then Gus and I began to peg, and the game ended with the old boys being left one to go out, and Gus having first count and pegging out on them. They wouldn't believe it. They laid all the hands out as they were played, and tried to find the place where Gus and I had cheated, but it was no go. Finally old Tready slammed the cards down and bellowed, "Where's that blooming tea?" and the door flew open and Mrs. Treadwell and Jessie came fluttering in with the tea and cakes.

I'd had enough cards by that time. I remembered I hadn't fed my dog, and said I thought I'd better be getting back in case he was hungry.

Of course Gus had to poke his oar in then. "Don't talk rot Mark," said he. "You fed him yesterday; I saw you myself." The old chaps both agreed it was a mistake to pamper a dog when he wasn't in regular work, so I had to sit down again. The next three games were a caution. I got that way at the finish I felt ashamed to pick up my hands; every one would be a 12 or 14 at least.

Gus gloated openly. He's about the most tactless man I know that way. After the seventh game Mr. Treadwell got up abruptly and kicked the girls' pet Persian cat from the front room clean out into the scullery. Then he stamped out after it, and we heard him out in the rain chopping wood.

Old Ginger pulled his chair up to the fire and said, "Hee! Hee! Easy seen you two chaps have played crib together before today."

After that Gus and I got our oilskins on and set off for home. It was getting dark, and we had two miles to plod, with the wind and rain in our faces. Every now and again I could hear Gus chuckling, so finally I said, "What's the joke? I can't see anything funny."

"I'm laughing at the way we beat those two old men," explained Gus.

"Yes," said I, "But if you'd let them win one or two, and kept them in a good humour, old Tready would have asked us to stop to tea. Now, when we get home, we've got to scratch about in the dark, chopping wood, and lighting our fire." That sobered Gus up when I put it that way. He said he'd never thought of that. Strikes me Gus never thinks of anything; a man ought to cut out going anywhere with him.

When we got home I cut some wood while Gus got kindling and layed the fire. We were just beginning to get personal to each other over whose turn it was to 'wash-up', when there came a rap at the door. I bellowed out, "Come in!" and in came Mr. Treadwell and Ginger. "We've come for our revenge," they announced.

I said I thought I had a touch of flu coming on, and felt I had better turn in, but nobody would hear of that. Tready said there was only one thing to do with influenza, and that was to beat it right from the start. If I gave in and lay down to it the chances were I'd end up in hospital. I use an old packing-case for a table at my house and benzine cases for chairs, and after the old chaps had tried all the furniture to see which were the least wobbly, old Ginger helped himself to a blanket off my bed to play on, and we made a start. We kept going till about 1 a.m., and every time the old chaps won a game they got unbearable. Every time they lost they developed cramp in the knees, through sitting with their knees doubled up against the packing case, and then they'd get up and stamp about the room, cursing my furniture. Finally Gus put the lid on things by referring to the tally of games, and saying, in a complacent voice, "Four you — eight us."

After letting us know that they weren't satisfied, and giving us the impression that there was something fishy about us they didn't like, they departed.

As soon as they were gone, I went to put my blanket back on the bed, and discovered a hole burnt in it as big as a soup plate where old Ginger had spilled ashes out of his pipe. It was carefully covered over with a piece of newspaper. "So that's where the smell of smouldering socks came from," said Gus, as soon as he saw it. "Never mind Mark, don't go so scotty about it. We beat them, that's the main thing."

It was fine the next day, so Gus and I did some work, but we were just finished tea that night when in came the two old boys again. They weren't satisfied. Gus was delighted, but I put my foot down. I said I had to go down to the township on business, and went and changed my clothes. They came in one at a time to try and persuade me to postpone the business, but it was important, and finally Gus nipped off and went for Arty Thompson. I drove about in the dark until a big shower came along and half-drowned me, and then I headed back home. They hardly bothered to grunt at me when I got inside, so I turned in.

They pounded the packing case with their fists, and passed remarks about the dealer every time they didn't get a decent hand until about 1:30 a.m., and after that Gus came chuckling into the bedroom, and I managed to get to sleep. Next night was the same, only Arty turned up with the other two, and I sat about behind the packing-case in the dark and cold until I was half-frozen, and then went to bed. Someone had commandeered my blanket again, and before I retired I caused a little excitement by going to the packing-case and dragging it off.

Gus said I was no sport at all if I allowed a small thing like that to upset me, but it was a cold, raw night, and I was firm. I heard them mumbling and muttering as I was shaking my bed up, but finally they settled down to the game again.

Instead of calling each other down every time their hands didn't suit, as they had done the night before, they expended all their superfluous breath in cursing the splinters in the packing-case and wishing they'd known I was that sort of man. About 1:30 again I rapped on the wall with my fist in order to command attention, while I informed them that Gus had blankets on his bed if a blanket was really necessary. After a long silence I heard a voice grumble, "Thought he was asleep long ago." Then I heard the benzine cases being pushed back and the card party broke up.

Next morning Gus broke the news to me. He and Arty had challenged Mr. Treadwell and Ginger to a crib tournament of a thousand games. They were going to play every evening during the winter until one side had won over 500, and the losers were to forfeit ten shillings each.

I asked Gus where they intended to play. "Oh! Here, of course," returned Gus, airily. "Can't expect Mrs. Treadwell or any of the women to clean up after us every night."

"And what about me?" I inquired mildly. "You?" exclaimed Gus, in surprise. "It needn't affect you. You don't have to play. I've gone to the trouble of getting Arty, because we saw you didn't care for crib."

Nearly every night for about three weeks the card enthusiasts mustered at my house, and helped themselves to a supper of tea and toast while they fought out the tournament.

Gus was in his glory. The competition excited outside interest, and another quartet annexed the box I used as a dressing table, and fought out a similar contest. As soon as the winners of the first 1000 games were decided the two losers were to take on the losers of the later party, while the winners played the winners. Every night my little kitchen was filled with a blue atmosphere of tobacco smoke, which used to drift in through the bedroom door and almost suffocate me.

Every morning the floor would be a litter of dead matches and pipe-dottles; but I didn't mind that so much. What I did object to was a habit old Ginger had of spitting at things lying about on the floor. I had to take my boots into the bedroom with me to finish up. And all the time they kept a roaring fire going of the wood I had carted home to see me through the winter. It was nothing to see eight of them leaning over a pack of cards at midnight, cutting, to see who would go out to chop a fresh back-log. Sometimes I would feel like sitting up by the fire for a bit, before turning into bed, but if I did that I was in the way, because Gus's party had their box drawn across the fireplace so that they could keep warm while they played. If I went to bed the opposition lot used to play their game up against the wall, about a foot from my head.

Our Quiet Winter

Once or twice I hinted gently that cards could be played without quite so much noise, but I found that only hurt their feelings.

I could see that they regarded me as a bit of a nuisance. I opened the back door once to let out some of the thick air, and the sudden draught blew all the lights out. They told me about that. Then, the evening before the tournament finally broke up, old Ginger went to the locker for a fresh candle and found only empty packets. He got quite cool over it. "You must have known there were no more there," he said to me. "What are we going to do now without lights?" "You're not doing anything, Mark," pointed out Mr. Treadwell, "nip over to Wilson's and borrow a packet."

It was getting near the deciding game. Gus and Arty were 485 games and Tready and Ginger had won 399. I began to work up a little interest in it myself.

The next evening they started early, and I hung about to see the finish. I squeezed myself into a small corner behind Gus and followed the game. About 11:30 Gus and his partner were 499, and things began to get exciting. As soon as the issue was beyond all doubt, Mr. Treadwell jumped up in a huff and accused Gus and Arty of playing with secret signs. Then old Ginger pointed a finger at me, where I sat crouched up in the corner, and said, "Look at him, too," in a nasty, sneery tone. The other lot of players stopped their game in order to hear the row. Gus and Arty could only sit and gape, so I said, "Look at me! What for?" "Ah! You needn't try and bluff it out," jeered Mr. Ginger. "I've been watching. I'm not as big a fool as you think. I suppose you and Tomlins think you're going to share the ten shillings, but you ain't. Hee, hee! We ain't that green." He and Mr. Treadwell made a dignified exit before Gus or I had thought out proper answers to him, and then I arose in my wrath and ordered the other party out of my house.

Gus and I finished the row by ourselves, and then Gus bundled his clothes into a sack, slammed my back door, and shook the dust of the place off his feet that same night.

The yarn got about that a party of hard affairs used to muster at my house all the winter, gambling for money, and that I was the ring-leader. Girls I thought I was friendly with started to give me the go-by, and even the old parson hunted me up to remonstrate. He said it wasn't the harm I did myself, but think of the dreadful wrong I was committing in coaxing young and innocent youths into the paths of gambling and ruin. Something like that it went. I hadn't even the heart to try and justify myself, but I did promise him that it would never happen again.

And it won't, either.

Gus and His Girl

One day I dropped in on old Gus Tomlins, and found him trying on a new tailor-made suit.

It was a pretty gorgeous affair, and I could see Gus had spread himself. The colour was a kind of bright blue, with a yellowish thread running through it and the pockets were cut at a queer slant and had spirals of little buttons on them. The slit at the back of the coat seemed to run up to the back of his neck and there were more spiral buttons on the sleeves. "Well, don't stand gaping there like a stuck pig," said Gus. "How does she fit?" I didn't answer him because I was too busy taking in all the details. Just where he should have had a few buttons, in my opinion, the tailor had run out, and made do with one. That was a fair sized one, and buttoned the waist coat together. The trousers were a work of joy and beauty forever. They had a seam down each side half an inch wide, turned up at the bottom, and the crease was absolutely startling. Gus got impatient and wanted to know my opinion of the turn out. I said it reminded me of a suit I saw once, when I was a boy. A Maori named Kahu lived close to us in those days, and after he had sold all his ancestral lands to the Pakeha and got cash down, he blossomed out in a suit like Gus's.

When I told Gus that, he gave a complacent smirk, and said now he was satisfied.

He said he could always tell when a thing really suited him, because I got envious, and showed by my manner that I begrudged him having it. As soon as I learned to curb my jealous nature and take a real disinterested friendly view, instead of running off into sarcasm, then he would take me into his confidence.

He laid out a pair of purple socks with green and silver parrots on them, as he spoke, and reached for a new silk tie, the colour of a fairly lively sunset.

Mark and Gus

I peeked about the room, and twigged new pointed boots, as yellow as bright varnish, and a new Stetson hat, that must have run into the best part of four quid on its own. "What's the trouble Gus?" said I. I was preparing to feel sorry for him. It struck me it must be the death of a dear one, at least, to cause Gus to go to such expense.

"Oh, well!" said Gus. "You don't understand, of course, Mark, but when a man has the privilege of knowing the nice kind of people I know, the least he can do is to turn out looking decent." Then I took a tumble. Gus had lost his head over some girl again, and hence the rig-out. I've seen Gus like this before, but never seen him run himself into thirty or forty quid over it, so I guessed it was a bad attack. I only hoped he would leave me out of it. I've had enough of getting into trouble trying to help him, but it was not to be. He said if I hadn't dropped in, he intended calling on his way down the road, because he wanted me to do him a small favour.

All he expected me to do was to turn up unexpectedly, at all sorts of odd hours and places, and take the girl's sister off his hands. It didn't appeal to me in the least. For one thing, the sort of girl that appeals to Gus always leaves me quite cold, and another thing, I'm finished with girls myself. I remember wasting over fifteen quid on clothes over a girl once, and it taught me a lesson. When Gus talks sensible, he can get anything out of me, and I gave in and decided to help him. He said he was going to take them into town to see the pictures, one in the side-car, and one on behind, and what he wanted me to do was to turn up before picture time, and hook on to the youngest. It interested me a bit, because I didn't happen to know either of them at the time, so I said all right, I would drive my gig into town and pick him up in the streets about half-past seven. Then I sat on his frowsy old bed, and watched him don his glad rags. He even had two handkerchiefs and a tin tie-pin, so I knew I was in for something.

When I got into town I spotted Gus and the two girls at once. Anyone could have picked him out a mile off, and it beat me how those two girls could stand there and appear unconscious, with a vision like that hurting their eyes. He was even carrying his overcoat instead of wearing it, so that nobody would miss anything. The sister I was to look after was rather a peach, and I felt sorry I hadn't put on my striped tie, as soon as I saw her. They greeted me with a kind of subdued curiosity, and I knew Gus had been telling them all about me. After Gus has given people a character sketch of me, it usually takes me a week or two to counterbalance it. They listen to Gus and then get the idea that I am simple and dull, but quite harmless.

The worst of it is, it's no use going snarky to Gus over it; he doesn't know he's leaving that impression. He thinks he's praising me up. I have a few stock phrases I always work off on girls, and then if they don't come to light, there's a loud silence.

The sister's name was Rosie. She seemed to think anything was better than that silence, and started to bubble and gurgle in an excited way, telling me about the ride into town on the motorbike. It appeared that Violet, that was the other one, had already had hysterics over a classy bit of steering Gus had treated them to. Rosie wanted to know did I think Mr. Tomlins was 'quite safe' with his machine. Personally, I don't think Mr. Tomlins is quite safe. I think he's 'damn dangerous', but I couldn't tell the girl that. I had to compromise, and said that if one of them came out with me it would ease the drag on the steering gear, and Gus would be able to handle his machine better. Gus and Violet were just on in front, and Rosie called them to put the proposition to them. Gus flashed a pleased and gratified look in my direction, and said it was just the very idea he had in his mind. Then the girls began to squabble about who should go with me. I setled myself resignedly to listen. It's always the same, as far as I'm concerned. I always have to take a back seat. For a time I was under the impression they were both anxious to go back in the side-car, and I think Gus had the same idea. Then it suddenly dawned on me that both Vi and Rosie were wrangling to dodge the side-car. Gus must have scared them pretty badly.

The girls finished their argument by hanging fondly on me, and asking if my gig wouldn't hold both of them.

Mark and Gus

I knew what it was going to be before I started. I never try to help Gus, but something like that crops up and spoils a man's day. I tried to tell them my gig wasn't safe, but they said they didn't mind, and they loved riding three in a gig, it was so cosy. Well, what could I do? Gus said I ought to have put my foot down and said "No", without my nonsense about it. But as I pointed out to him, who was to know they'd come at a thing like that? It caught me unprepared, and I had agreed to take the both of them before I knew where I was. Then we went to the pictures, and whenever I was lucky enough to forget Gus for a while, I enjoyed myself. When the lights went up I caught Gus eyeing me with a 'how could you' sort of expression. I felt uncomfortable, but anyhow, why should he always be the big man when we went together anywhere.

It was a new experience for me being sought after like that, and I decided to make the most of it. After the show was over, I suggested we had some tea and cakes, and I had to give Vi the tip to invite Gus in, because he was slinking off into the darkness. That perked him up a bit, when she ran after him, and we had a fairly lively snack in the tea shop. If Gus hadn't got personal, and said what a pity I couldn't keep my sleeve out of the butter when I reached for things, all might have ended quite all right for him. But as soon as he said that, Vi stuck up for me and said it was an accident. Then Gus went on, and said it wasn't an accident at all, I had a habit of doing it, and whenever he took me out anywhere, it was always the same. So then I had to point out that he was stirring his tea with the sugar spoon, and he slung the spoon on his plate and got up and stamped out. I get out of patience with Gus sometimes. There was no need for him to make such an exhibition of himself, it reflected on me, being seen with a man like that. The girls giggled until he had got outside, and then Vi said she felt sorry for him, but he deserved it for giving them such a fright when he fetched them into town. They weren't half so chummy on the road back, and a dark suspicion entered my mind that I was Mr. Juggins, and that they were playing me off against Gus just to play him out. That sort of thing doesn't appeal to me at all. I decided to give

Gus and His Girl

Gus the tip about them when I saw him next day. When I told Gus my ideas about it he brightened up visibly, and said, "By jove, Mark, you're right. What a mug I was to take any notice. A man might have known no girl would take a liking to you." That's all the thanks I got for trying to open his eyes about them, and about half an hour later I heard his old bus tearing down the road at top speed. Next day he was over again, and had more proposals to put to me. He said he was taking them to the Ngaere Gardens on Sunday, and he had promised Rosie I would be there as well. I told him he had better go back and tell Rosie I had the "flu", because I wasn't going to waste a good Sunday at Ngaere Gardens for her, or all the girls in Taranaki. It ended up by me giving in, as usual. Gus said Rosie would be sure to be hurt if I didn't turn up, she had been talking about me ever since the night at the pictures. I said, "All right, I don't want to disappoint the poor kid, if she's set on me coming."

I bought a new straw hat for that outing, and wore my best tie. I'm glad now I didn't go any further, because twice I walked into a shop after brown boots, and sneaked out again before the attendant saw me. It would have been a sheer waste of good money, as things turned out. Gus took the girls to Ngaere with his turnout, and I drove through later on in my gig. The first slap in the eye I got, was when Rosie spotted me. She said, "Hullo! We didn't expect to see you here today." She may have suffered disappointment if I hadn't turned up, but if she was pleased to see me she hid it pretty well. I registered a silent resolve to let Gus go on his way in future. If that girl talked about me to Gus after I took her to the pictures, all I can say is she made up for it at Ngaere that day, because she wouldn't even talk at me when I got there.

Gus was in great fettle. He had discarded the purple socks with the parrots on them, and was showing three or four inches of a kind of sickly fawn, with white and brown clocks. That sort of clobber always makes me shiver, but girls seem to like it. I had to follow the three of them round, while they giggled and nudged each other, and if I fell back behind, Gus would turn round and shake me up about it. "Come on, Mark, old man, don't lag like that," he'd say, "let's all enjoy ourselves." Then he'd gush off about the beautiful tints on Mt. Egmont, just as if he'd never seen it before, instead of living on its slopes for about four years. I do hate a man that can't be natural. Then he had another go at me — said I seemed silent—hadn't said a word hardly since I arrived. So I pulled myself together, and said the cloud on the mountain was drifting this way, and it looked like rain. There was a screech at that, and Gus explained that I had a habit of trying to put the damper on, but nobody was to take any notice of me, I couldn't help being like that. About half an hour after, the first drops of rain fell, and then the girls scuttled for shelter. They had on a kind of pinkish frock, with a lacy net work affair over it, so that the pink showed through. I must say they looked pretty fine. Gus kept staring out and calling it a sunshower, in a cheery, optimistic tone, but it got worse and worse, and pretty soon it was raining cats and dogs. The girls were chiefly concerned about their dresses, but they managed to let Gus know in between whiles that they considered the rain was his fault. Girls are mighty queer things to have anything to do with, I can see that. I had to feel sorry for old Gus myself, because he didn't order the shower, I'll bet anything on that. The only thing for everybody to do seemed to be to go home, so Gus and I tucked them safely into the sidecar, one sitting on the other's lap, and covered them over with a couple of clean sacks I had managed to secure. Then Gus began to sweat and mutter at his bike, and couldn't get it to go. I told him straight, if I had a bike like that I'd burn it — couldn't he see he was getting the girls wet through, keeping them out in the rain the way he was doing. Finally, I harnessed up my horse, and they decided to go with me. A pool of water had collected on the sack the girls were crouched under, and Gus poured about a pint of it down Vi's neck before he noticed it. For a nice girl, she had a fair amount to say about it — I was glad I liked Rosie best. I got about two miles towards home, when Gus came roaring and panting along, and it was decided to transfer the girls again, because they would get home quicker, and get into the dry. They made the shift pretty dejectedly, said it didn't really matter, their dresses were ruined anyhow.

Then Gus buzzed away, and I settled that was my last appearance as a ladies' man. In future, I was going to walk round a corner if I saw a girl coming towards me even. How people can rave about Ngaere Gardens beats me properly.

They say, "Take the girl to Ngaere Gardens," but once was going to be enough for me.

When I got within a mile of Stratford, I looked through the mist ahead and noticed a crowd gathered on a bend in the road. It was three people, and as I drew nearer, I picked them out to be Gus and his passengers. The girls were sitting on a grassy bank, sobbing and pulling barberry prickles out of hands and arms, and Gus was trying to back his turnout out of a barberry hedge. He had been so keen to get the girls home out of the wet, that he had taken the corner at top speed, and the extra weight in the side-car had prevented the old bus coming round properly. I knew something like that would happen to him, sooner or later. The man absolutely asks for it. I asked him why he hadn't put his brake on when he found she wouldn't answer the helm, instead of barging the poor girls into a prickly hedge in that silly way. That's a thing I've noticed about Gus. As soon as you point out where he's wrong, he gets excited. There was no need for him to swear in front of the girls either. I only asked him a simple question.

The girls had to get into the gig again, and I towed Gus and his rotten turnout behind. Everybody stared at us as we went through Stratford, and the girls started to get snappy. They said they'd never been made such an exhibition of in all their lives, and as soon as they got home, we were never to attempt to speak to them again. Never! Violet had the skin peeled off her nose, and Rosie had a black eye, where a twig had nearly poked it out. I noticed the rain and tears had made tracks down their cheeks, and a suspicion struck me they weren't as pretty as I thought they were.

I never want to speak to them again myself, they gave me quite enough of their company on that drive home. To hear them talk, one would almost fancy Gus and I had gone in league against them, and that we had mapped out the whole programme before we started. That's what I tell Gus. Never try to do a girl a favour. Look at the way I waited on those two with my horse and gig, and as soon as I drew up at their gate, they flounced out and tore up the path with their noses in the air.

Never so much as good-bye to either Gus or me. One thing about it, old Gus has got to the simple life again, and a man can be seen in his company now. The last I saw of the fancy socks, he was wearing them with his milking clobber, and the queer suit has been put away some where. But I'm afraid it's only temporary, because the other day I asked him why he didn't wear it for a working suit, and he nearly had a fit. "That suit! Good lor', man! What on earth next? That's me best suit."

Gus Buys a Bull

One day I went round to the sale-yards, to see how stock was selling, and who should I see up on the rails but old Gus Tomlins.

"Come on, Mark," he shouted, "I'm going in for pedigree Jerseys. You know a little about bulls. Let's have the benefit of your knowledge."

I climbed up on the rail beside him, and viewed the stuff below. Gus was on the waver as to which of two bulls he would bid for. He wanted my opinion, but I wasn't having any. I helped him buy a jibbing horse once, and although my part in the business was advising him not to buy, he has forgotten that, and reproaches me about that horse every time he thinks of it.

My idea about buying things is to use your own judgement, and not go running round to all your friends, trying to put the responsibility on to them. I told Gus that, and he said certainly it was his money, and he intended to suit himself, but there was no need for me to stop like a deaf mute about it, I could express my opinion without hurting anybody.

I remembered hearing a man say once that a fine tail was a good sign in Jersey stuff, so I pointed out the bull with the finest tail, and said I fancied him.

"Him!" said Gus. "Where's your eyes, man? Look at this other fellow. Better class of bull all round."

I knew that's how it would be. I never know anything. I drew Gus's attention to the tail, but he had some facts about depth of neck, straightness of back, and so on, and floored me completely.

Gus is about the greatest man for collecting that sort of knowledge that ever I knew. It's a marvel to me he isn't a millionaire by now, the useful things he knows. He can discourse scientifically on any branch of farming you like to open out on, and he admits himself that the only thing that keeps him back is lack of capital. If he only had a few thousands to work on he'd show people how to make money.

He finally bought the bull his own fancy declared the best, and after he had made arrangements with a drover to get it out home that night, we went up town and had a drink to celebrate the bargain. Gus said it was a good job he hadn't taken any notice of me — he would have been landed in the soup if he'd bought the thing I fancied.

He said he had a bundle of old papers over at his place, and if I liked, he would lend them to me, and I could study the pictures and get an idea of 'type'.

All great breeders relied on 'type' to sell their stock and it would pay me to study it up a bit. Perhaps I might want to buy a pedigree bull myself some day, and he wouldn't always be about to help me. As a matter of fact, Gus said, he had an idea he might sell out pretty shortly and go up Auckland way; he thought there was more 'scope' for a good judge of stock up that way. In Gus's opinion Taranaki was about played out, every little farmer fancied himself as a pedigree man and real sound knowledge and judgement wasn't appreciated. I drew Gus's attention to the fact that I had bought a pedigree bull two years ago, and he said, "Eh? Oh, that!" and then went on about what a pity it was he hadn't been there at the time. "They'd never have landed you with that scarecrow if I'd been there, Mark."

Up till then I had always been rather proud of that bull of mine. To hear Gus talk like that hurt my feelings, and I had to tell him "at least my bull was quiet". The bull Gus had just purchased looked anything but quiet to me. Gus said, "Pooh! I'll put a ring in his nose tomorrow, and after he has been tied up a day or two and fed on hay, I'll have him like a sheep." He proceeded to make plans about ringing the bull.

I was to come over after dinner and help him drive the bull across to my stockyard and we would ring him there. I had arranged to meet an uncle of mine that day, but Gus said that would be all right; he'd square Tom Wilson to go and meet the mail train and my uncle could come up with Tom.

Gus Buys a Bull

My uncle John is getting a bit old and faddy, and I like to humour the old chap if I can, so I thought it would be better if Gus put the job off for a day, and let me meet the old man myself.

To hear Gus growling and mumbling anyone would have thought it was his uncle and that he didn't want him, but I was firm. If a man has relations coming to see him the least he can do is to make them welcome.

Another thing, Uncle John has three or four farms down on the good land, Hawera way, and has often told me he thinks it a pity I wasn't on land like his, down there.

He has it leased at present, but that's no reason why I should go out of my way to wound the old chap's feelings. I went down to get uncle myself. He had a bottle of whisky in his coat pocket, and another in his bag.

I must say he's a game old sport, for an old man. Gus and I sat up with him till 3 a.m., listening to his hair-raising yarns about the "good old days". If we hadn't mopped up all the old chap's whisky he'd never have gone to bed.

One thing about old Gus, he never fails a man. Any time Uncle John is due, I give Gus the wire and he ambles along to help me get rid of the whisky. That's the only way I can handle the old boy at all. Dispose of his liquid refreshments and he generally fills in one day getting over the journey, and then has important business calling him away.

I always turn my bed over to Uncle John and doss on cow-covers and a heap of hay, but he is too old to really appreciate the sacrifice. He just takes it for granted I always sleep in the corner on that heap of hay.

I got up at 6 a.m. the morning after uncle arrived and went out to get my cows in. I didn't hear Gus over the way, so I had to slip over and give him a call. Gus was fast asleep and when I shook him and said, "Come on Gus, you're half an hour late," he broke out with a dismal groan. I felt a bit seedy myself somehow or other, but work had to be done. Gus told me that morning that if he had an uncle like my Uncle John, he'd buy a gun. I could see he must be feeling pretty low to talk about a man's relations like that. I got back from the factory about half past nine, and all the way home I was picturing the fire Uncle John would have lit, and the nice cup of tea that would be all ready for me. I spotted the chimney when I was still half a mile off, but couldn't see any smoke.

I whipped old Bloss up, a man never knows when these old chaps are going to turn it in, and it struck me Gus might have to wait another day to ring his bull after all. It was all right, as it happened, Uncle John hadn't woke up, that was all.

I left him in bed while I fried some steak and made the tea, and when I had his breakfast fixed up on a clean plate I took it in. I took a lot of trouble over that breakfast. I know Uncle John doesn't like black fingermarks on the crockery, or verdigris on the fork, and I polished everything up with the dish cloth for him, but it was labour wasted. He sat up in bed with a look of incredulous horror. "Steak! Steak in the morning! Hang it! What did I think he was? A crocodile!" I didn't think anything of the sort, but I could see it was no use arguing, so I took the feed out again and ate it myself. Then the old boy climbed out and poured tea over everything, trying to refill his cup, and I went away to feed the calves. He wobbled out after a while and showed me all the calves that had weak constitutions. He said I might just as well knock them on the head because any fool could see they'd never see the winter through. I had been feeding them for about two months, so I decided to keep on and take a sporting chance about it.

Uncle John brightened up a little after dinner and said he would help Gus and me to ring the bull. We went over to Gus's place and found Gus looking rather yellow. Uncle gave him a lecture about it. Uncle wanted to know why he didn't use his common sense; if he suffered from biliousness, why didn't he go to the seat of the trouble and doctor himself up. By the looks of him Uncle reckoned it was diseased liver he had and he would have to be very, very careful of himself. He should go down to Hawera and see some quack down there Uncle knew, and if anything could be done, that would be the man to do it. Gus led the way inside, and here Uncle had some more to say.

When he was a young man he bached in a tin shanty for years and people used to come from far and near in order to see how clean and neat he kept his things.

He said Gus's house was a filthy, revolting sight, not fit for pigs, let alone human beings. How a strong, husky young man like Gus could be content to wallow in such loathsome circumstances had Uncle beat properly.

"Look at the floor! Good heavens, man! Don't you ever scrape it!"

Gus got a bit huffy, the way Uncle John kept harping on, and snapped, "No, I don't scrape it, I sweep it." Gus said it was all very fine for some people to come nosing about where they weren't wanted, and pull things to pieces, but when a man was running a dairy farm single handed, he had other work to do. If Gus started messing about the house, getting finicky over things, who was going to do the work? Uncle roared again at that. Uncle said nobody expected him to live in the place all the time, but why didn't he clean the show up, say once a week.

He asked Gus for the broom, and said he would give him an idea of what he meant. Gus had to hunt about a bit before he found it, and finally I remembered we had used it out in his shed a fortnight ago, to sweep up a bag of slag that had burst, when Gus was preparing to drill in his spring oats. When Gus got back with the broom, Uncle John started to sweep up. He dived into corners that hadn't been swept for four years, and the rubbish he collected was a caution.

Gus put in an anxious time hopping to and fro over the broom, rescuing studs and lost pipes and little things he'd lost the run of for years.

I enjoyed the show, myself. It was a change to see Gus getting bowled out so neatly, because he always puts on such side when he comes over to see me. To hear Gus criticizing my housekeeping, a stranger would fancy he'd come straight out of a palace, and I was pleased to see him taken down a peg. Uncle took the cream off the joke, however. He leaned on his broom for a while to let the dust settle, and said that only once in all his experience had he ever seen anything approaching it.

Mark and Gus

I wanted to keep the old chap on the subject — it isn't often I get such a good one on to old Gus — so I said, in an eager voice, "And when was that, Uncle John?" Uncle John looked me up and down, in a calm, impartial manner and replied, "Over at that stinking hovel of yours, me lad." After that Gus and I left the old chap to it, and went out to muster the bull.

Gus wondered if old Uncle had always been so insulting. He said it was a funny thing to him that he had reached such a green old age. We finally decided it was rot to take any notice of him. He was in his second childhood, and men like us should humour the old chap and pretend we really liked listening to him. Gus said he expected I would be the same long before I reached Uncle John's age, because he noticed a tendency to nag about me, even now. Evidently it ran in my family. We drafted Gus's pedigree bull out on to the road, and ran him over to my yard with a couple of yearlings for company.

Gus had the ring, and I supplied a coil of rope, and a steel to drill the hole with. Uncle John turned up before we had any thing fixed, and proceeded to take the situation in hand. As the bull was nervous — not wild, just nervous — Uncle showed us how to tell a wild bull from a nervous one. We decided to throw him down and tie his legs. The one thing every man had to be careful about in ringing a bull, was to be sure and not lose the small screw that fastened the ring together after it was through the nose. Gus trusted me with it; he said he would fix the ring in place, and when he held his hand out, I was to put the screw into his fingers. Then there would be no mistakes. One thing we all hated, especially Uncle John, was a mess up over a job like that. The reason Uncle John reckoned the bull was nervous was because he ran round and round the yard, trying all the spaces between the rails. If he were out and out wild it would be a different tale. We wouldn't be in that yard with him, Uncle John could tell us that. We weren't in that yard with him very much longer as it happened, because when Gus coiled up the rope and made a move to lassoo him, things began to happen. Uncle John bit his clay pipe through while he was climbing the rails, and the way he went off about it was a fair scorcher.

Gus Buys a Bull

Gus said he would buy him a gross of the things if he would only shut up, but that was no good. That clay pipe was the only one Uncle had ever managed to colour properly in fifty years' experience with clay pipes. He wouldn't have taken ten pounds for it, and there it was smashed, all because Gus didn't have the brains to know a wild bull when he saw one. Next time Uncle came to help us he was going to have things done his way, or else he would go inside out of it, and let us get killed our own way — he didn't care which.

When Gus left the yard he forgot to take the rope with him and we had a bit of an argument as to who would get down off the rails and get it.

I would have done it myself, only as I pointed out to Gus, he was careless enough to leave it there, so it was up to him to go back for it.

We finally compromised by raking it through the rails with the aid of a garden rake lashed to the end of a long pole. One of the little things I've been intending to do for the last year or so, is to build a strong race in my yard, so that I can run wild cattle into it and shut them in. We put in over an hour trying to snare that bull from the rails, and finally Uncle John got impatient and took the rope away from us. He coiled it up in two neat coils and held it in one hand, with two fingers separating the coils. That was the proper way to hold a lariat.

As soon as the bull turned his head towards Uncle he shouted, "Now watch closely, boys," and threw the whole thing at the bull.

It landed on his horns, and if Uncle had only hung on to one end, instead of letting the whole lot go, he would have saved us a lot of worry. After the bull had shaken it off, and made a careful examination of it, it was Uncle's turn to get the rope, but the old chap jibbed on it. He said he wouldn't have minded going down into the yard with that bull, if Gus and I had only done what he wanted us to do at first. Now the bull was excited, after the way we had been messing around with him, and Uncle said our stupid folly was the cause of it, and we could finish the job ourselves. We raked the rope out again, and before we tried any more lassoo work, we tied one end to the top rail of the yard, and then I had a go. I used to be pretty good at that sort of thing once.

I remember lassooing our big rooster at home once, when I was a boy. He was just in the deep notes of a very impressive crow, when I got him round the neck, and everybody that spotted him for the next week or so thought some dog had worried him. I must have lost my throw since then, because I didn't make much of a show at snaring the bull. Gus did the trick in the end, and then he started to tell Uncle John and I why it was we had been so long over it.

If we'd only let him do it, instead of insisting on having a go ourselves, the bull would have been rung hours ago. If we wanted to practise that sort of thing, why didn't we practise on a post somewhere in the evenings, instead of wasting valuable time when he wanted to get his pedigree bull rung. The next job was to throw the bull and get him tied up securely. That didn't take very long, because we hauled him up to a post, and then got down into the yard and surrounded him. Uncle John got kicked in the watch-pocket, while he was stooping down explaining to Gus how to make a slip knot, and lay it on the ground for the bull to step into.

I thought the old chap was done that time. I remembered wondering who would be responsible for the funeral expenses, while I was nipping to the house for a billy of water. The old boy was only winded, luckily, and after I had heaved the water over him, he soon let us know he wasn't dead. While he went away to pack his swag up, Gus and I threw the bull and ringed him.

I remembered the little screw, and put it in my mouth for safety.

I was leaning over Gus to see he did things right, when the bull made a desperate struggle for liberty, and Gus's head came up and caught me in the face. I spat blood, and cried, and blew my nose, for about half a minute and then Gus got wild because

Gus Buys a Bull

I couldn't find that little screw. It was getting near milking time, and we fixed things in the end by reaving a fine piece of wire through the bull ring, and twisting the ends.

Gus said of all the born fools, I was one of them. Next time he had a little job to do I was to keep away, I only got in his road and worried him. I don't see there was any need for that, myself.

If he'd kept his head still, instead of jerking it about the way he did, I wouldn't have swallowed the screw. I told him the best thing he could do was to lose his fool of a bull and lead it away out of my yard. I didn't want it on my place.

Gus calmed down and talked more reasonably after that. He said it was only an accident, and I shouldn't get so touchy over it.

Nobody could help that sort of thing happening, it was just fate, and he expected it would be better to leave the bull tied up in the yard for a day before we shifted him.

He thought if I gave him some hay and a drink of water, he would be quite all right, and we could get him home next day when he was calmed down a bit more.

Then we went inside to see what time it was, and had to inspect Uncle John's gold watch. Uncle had it all spread out on a newspaper, and how a bull could kick a watch to pieces like that in one kick beat me.

It was a family heirloom that watch, no money could have bought it, and Uncle John gave us its whole history. He said he had intended leaving it to me, together with a few other of his small belongings, but now I could welter in poverty where I was.

Every time I woke up in the future and remembered that I didn't have that watch, I could just meditate on the way I had smashed it up on him. He said once he used to feel sorry for me, dragging out a poverty stricken existence, on such a sour, barren farm. He had intended seeing what he could do about it, some of his Hawera land would be on his hands again shortly, but now he was going to wash his hands of me.

He was finished with me. He came up to give me a helping hand, knowing I would be busy, and I deliberately set out to show him he wasn't wanted. Gus dodged away to get his cows in, and I went for mine, and when I got inside again that night, Uncle John had gone, bag and baggage.

Next morning Gus came over to take his bull home, and tried to tell me it was all my fault — I knew what Uncle John was like, and Gus said I should have taken precautions to see the poor old chap didn't get hurt. The bull was still too wild to lead and Gus seemed to fancy that it was my fault as well.

He said it seemed queer to him, the way that bull played up, if anyone went near him. Almost as if he had been knocked about.

I didn't like the suspicious way Gus looked at me when he said that. I asked him if he thought I'd spent the night prodding his bull with a stick, and Gus said, "Oh, no, no, only, he shouldn't be as wild as that."

Gus had seen hundreds of bulls ringed and tied up for a night, and they had all tamed down by morning.

We tied a post on to the end of the chain in the finish, and then let the bull out, and he dragged that post over to Gus's place by his nose. He made pretty good time, too, and if he hadn't got the post jammed across Gus's calf paddock gate when he bolted through there, I doubt if we could have caught him again. Gus tied him up to the fence, and then expressed himself as satisfied. "Mark," he said, "it's a good job it was me who bought this bull. You would never have handled him if you'd got him." Not a word of credit for me or Uncle John.

A man ought to cut out trying to help Gus Tomlins.

Violet Again

Every time Gus Tomlins gets a new idea into his head he inflicts himself on me for an hour or so, while he tells me all about it.

I was just filling up my pipe after tea one evening, when he dropped in to see me. After carefully dusting the top of a seat — a thing he wouldn't dream of thinking of in his own house — he sat down, and gazed in silence at the fire.

"What's up? Toothache?" I enquired, after I had stuck it as long as I could.

Gus looked up. "Mark," he said, "Has it ever struck you what a senseless, low habit smoking is?"

I got such a shock that my pipe fell down the front of my shirt, where I had it open at the neck, and after all the excitement was over, I had forgotten what Gus said.

He came back to the subject again, however, but I was more prepared, next time. "Don't talk silly nonsense," I told him. "Everybody smokes nowadays."

"Yes," said Gus, "That's just it, and look at the way the human race is deteriorating." I tried to convince him that it was white bread, instead of brown, that was doing the damage, but it was no use.

And another thing, Gus reckoned, look at the run we'd get with the girls. None of the fair sex really liked the smell of tobacco. I said that as far as I was concerned, it would have to be a case of mutual tolerance. I didn't like seeing a girl all decked up with paints and powders, but I put up with it, and it was up to them to do the same about tobacco.

That was silly talk, Gus said. There was no comparison at all. One grain of nicotine was enough to kill a dog, but a man could eat a bucketful of powder, without being inconvenienced. He spoke with such assurance about the powder, that I could see he was at home on that subject anyhow. Finally he began to be overbearing and sarcastic. Said I wouldn't try to uplift myself, because I was a drug fiend. Tobacco had me down. I got a bit annoyed with him before it was all over, and the finish of it was that I challenged him to a wager for ten shillings, that I could keep off smoking longer than he could. We shook hands on that. Gus seemed to think that neither of us would ever want to smoke again, after making that bet. He suggested that I lessen any temptation that might assail me, by collecting all my pipes and tobacco, and burning them then and there.

I drew the line at that. I had nearly a pound of flake-cut on hand, and it seemed too much like waste to me. "Mark," said Gus, in a hushed voice, some time after we had made our decision, "If it hadn't been for Violet, I'd never have known how low a habit it really was. It's wonderful —" he mused, "The uplifting influence of a really fine woman."

"Violet!" I almost shouted. "So she's in this, is she?" If I'd only known Miss Vi had any hand in influencing Gus to stop smoking, he'd never have inveigled me into that silly bet. I thought he really meant to try and improve himself, the way he led up to the subject, and here it was, only a girl, after all. I tried to wriggle out of the bet, as soon as I found that out, but Gus wouldn't hear of it. Gus said that Violet considered a man who smoked a pipe to be a revolting spectacle, and the smell of stale tobacco nearly always made her feel faint.

There was to be a dance down at the township in a week's time, and all he wanted me to do was to mention to Vi, in a casual, matter-of-fact tone, that Gus had sworn off tobacco. He said I had better tell her about myself too. It wouldn't hurt any, because then he could claim the credit for converting me as well. And there was no danger of Violet taking a fancy to a man like me, even if I was a non-smoker. I said, "Why not mention it to her yourself?" but Gus thought if he did that, it might seem like swank, whereas if she got it second hand she couldn't help but be impressed. I promised to do my best, and then Gus went home, and I buried all my tobacco and pipes down at the bottom of my clothes chest, and went to bed.

Next morning my Big Ben went off as usual, and I sat up and reached for my pipe. It wasn't there, of course, so then I lit a match and searched the floor, under the impression I'd knocked it off the box during the night. Then I remembered

Violet Again

Gus and the bet. It occurred to me that if Mr. Gus stopped home a bit more, instead of annoying people three or four nights a week by calling to explain every rotten idea that struck him, life might be pleasanter. But a bet's a bet, so I had a drink of water, and went for the cows. By the time I had finished milking, and was harnessing up, ready to go to the factory, I was so hungry that I could almost have eaten the horse. All the way down the road, I kept changing the reins from one hand to the other, while I went through my pockets. I knew I'd put my smoking materials carefully away the night before, but that didn't seem to affect my hands. Gus was already there, when I arrived, and was standing up in his cart, gazing thoughtfully into space.

His hands were moving slowly about, tapping every pocket, and as soon as I noticed that, I felt more satisfied. I strolled over to speak to him. No! He'd never even had a hankering for a smoke that morning, he told me. It was just a matter of willpower. He'd decided to chuck the habit, and that settled it. Arty Thompson came over and held out a cigarette, and Gus's hand went out.

I let out a yell, and Gus's hand flew back again. "What's the use of blaring like that?" he demanded. "Couldn't you see I was only waving it away?" The testy tone he adopted got on my nerves, and I had to tell him to keep his temper.

It wasn't him, Gus reckoned, it was me. For a touchy, irritable man I took the biscuit.

If he ever got as liverish as me, he said, he'd take something for it.

A benign, fatherly old chap in glasses, who was standing waiting his turn near us, heard the argument, and bustled cheerily over.

"Liver, Mark? You try a pinch of Epsom salt in your tea every morning." I was glad to get away from that factory. Everybody there seemed as if they knew I'd stopped smoking, and were having a sly leer at me. Gus said afterwards, that he felt the same way. Every time he met a milk-cart on his road home he half expected them to pull up and shout, "Ha Ha! Gus, where's your pipe?" I went over to Gus's place that same morning, to borrow some bread I had forgotten to get at the store, and found Gus in his calf paddock. He was chasing his pet pedigree calf around with a long rail, trying to brain it. I knew exactly how he felt, because I had given my old horse a hiding myself, just a short time before, for trying to back in and knock down my milk stand on purpose, when I went to unload the cans.

Gus threw the rail down, when he saw me, and said, "I don't know how it is, Mark, but every blessed thing has gone wrong today." The same thing had happened with me, so we sat down and compared notes. I suggested it was lack of the soothing influence of tobacco, and something would have to be done about it. If it got any worse, I could see that Gus and I would end our promising careers up at New Plymouth Breakwater, cracking stones, because we wouldn't be able to kill off all our livestock without someone hearing about it, and putting us away. I wanted to cry off the bet, and try again next year say, when we might be more used to the idea, but Gus got filled with a noble indignation at the mere thought. He said the very difficulties in the way were a help and an encouragement to him.

No great reform was ever carried through without a struggle. He implied that I was like the fellow he'd heard or read about, some time or other, and waved his hand at me, and said: "Get thee behind me, Mark." I asked him what use that was going to do, and then he said it was a quotation.

"Look here Gus," I told him, "You needn't start slinging poetry at me just because you had a year at high school. I won't have it."

We both started getting personal and reminding each other of all the favours we'd done each other, and finally Gus came off his high horse and said: "This is no good Mark. I'll tell you what. We'll go inside, and have just one smoke."

As soon as old Gus said that, I began to wonder what on earth we had been snapping about, and we both went into Gus's kitchen.

Violet Again

I shifted a pile of mouldy potato and onion peelings off a chair and sat down while Gus got out the tobacco, and two pipes. While we were smoking the pipe of peace, I thought of Vi, and said: "What will Violet think of this?" Gus got such a shock that he knocked the packet of flake-cut off the end of the table into a bucket that stood on the floor, with his house milk in it. He scooped the tobacco out carefully, using the greasy old sardine tin he uses to pick up eggs, out of the frying pan, and hoped tobacco didn't affect cream rising, or he would have to cut out his morning porridge, because porridge was no good to him without cream. By that time he had collected his thoughts, and said: "Violet! Why should she know? Why tell her anything about it?"

He glared angrily at me, but when a thing touches my personal honour, I can take a firm stand.

I told him it wouldn't be honourable for me to act a lie like that, especially to a girl. "But this isn't a smoke, man," declared Gus, blowing out a cloud, and waving his pipe at me. "It's medicine. It's for our nerves. You don't suppose —" he ended accusingly, "I'm enjoying this do you?" Just shows how a man can be mistaken. When Gus put it that way, I saw his point of view, and came round. He said we could allude to it as a 'tonic'. All drug victims had to resort to tonics, in order to still the cravings when they were being cured, and there was nothing dishonest about it, if we looked at it in that way. "One thing," said I, "We've both smoked, so the bet's off." Gus had to reluctantly admit that, but contended that it was up to me to see him through, just the same. He generously suggested that I could have a tonic, every time my nerves felt frayed, but I wasn't to degenerate back into a pipe fiend, because he wanted to impress Vi with the fact that his good example had reformed me. It's no good being mates with a chap, if you aren't prepared to help him, and I couldn't see any serious inconvenience to myself, so long as no restrictions were placed on the 'tonics', so I gave in.

The pot was boiling, so Gus said I had better stop to dinner.

Mark and Gus

Dinner at Gus's place is never anything to rave about. I generally have a tin of golden syrup at my show, if any visitor drops in, but all Gus ever provides, besides bread and butter, is half a pot of bloater paste. He puts it in front of the visitor with —"Here y'are. I never eat it, but you might care for some," and then sails into his bread and butter.

I've seen that pot of paste a good many times in the last year or so, but no visitor has ever been game enough to have a go at it yet.

I wonder he bothers to mention it at all when I'm dining with him. He knows how I feel about it, but I suppose it's his colonial hospitality. The dance down at the township was Gus's chief concern.

I was to be sure and dance with Vi as soon as I got there, and mention about the tobacco. "How am I to know the girl will dance with me?" I demanded. "The last time I saw Violet, she and Rosie were giving us instructions never to speak to them again." "That's all right," explained Gus, "I've squared that long ago."

He suggested that I went with him in the side-car, but I said it didn't matter. I thought I'd sooner drive down in the gig, it would keep my horse from getting too fresh. I've been bit too often, going with Gus.

He has a habit of sneaking up to me just before the last dance, and saying, "I say, Mark old man, do us a favour, will you?"

That means I've got to walk home, while Gus takes some girl home in the side-car. Gus got down to the dance before I did, on the night, and as soon as I put in an appearance, he began to pester me to go in and dance with Violet.

I always feel a bit nervous starting off at a dance. My way is to wait until a dance is called out, and then mingle with the crowd and drift in. Gus seemed to think I ought to rush straight in, and book a dance right off, but I wasn't having any. Presently I managed to screw up enough courage, however, and approached Violet diffidently. In spite of Gus's assurance, I wasn't so sure myself she'd recognize me. She was pretty cool the last time I'd seen her, when I'd driven her back from Ngaere gardens. She greeted me with a gracious smile, so I knew it was all serene, and engaged her for the next dance. As soon as the music started we commenced dancing. She was chatting away, and the dance must have been half over, before I remembered Gus's instructions. I cast about in my mind how to broach the subject, and finally asked her if she smelt any stale tobacco smoke about me.

Her eyes nearly popped out of her head with surprise, at such a change of subject, because I'd been admiring her dress, and the new way she had her hair fixed before that.

"No, why?" she asked. Then I told her about how Gus and I had turned over a new leaf, and stopped smoking.

She seemed to ponder, for a while, and then said: "What a strange idea. I simply love to see men smoking, they always look so contented." After that I changed the subject again. I wondered what on earth old Gus had been dreaming about, and decided to give him a piece of my mind.

As soon as the dance was over, I got him in a corner, and explained what had happened.

It had Gus puzzled completely. "But look here Mark, she called it a nasty, low habit," he said.

"Well, she's changed her views," I told him. "You'd better hustle your mind along, and change yours."

"I'm having the next waltz with her," he said, "I'd better not mention smoking at all."

We both lit up, and Gus said what a lucky thing it was that we had remembered to bring our pipes along. Then Gus went in for his dance. As Violet was so fond of seeing men smoking, there was no need for me to conceal myself, and I stood at the porch door, peering in at the dancers, and puffing away at my pipe. Gus told me what happened afterwards. As soon as Vi saw him, she asked in a sweet, kindly way how he ever managed without tobacco.

He would have laughed it off, only he didn't get a chance to reply. She went on to say what a fine thing it was, to see two young men trying to uplift themselves the way we were doing. It showed great strength of character, and nobility of mind.

Before Gus realized it, he was following her lead, and explaining to her how we had both put our pipes away, and were stilling the tobacco craving with 'tonics'. Just then they waltzed past the porch door, and Violet stared point blank into my face as she went by.

"Your friend evidently kept one pipe out," she told Gus. Then Gus disowned me. He told Violet that if I'd do a thing like that, after all the trouble he'd taken over me, I wasn't worth bothering about any more. They both agreed that there was something funny about me they didn't like, and then the dance stopped, and Gus escorted her to a seat.

Gus struck one of his attitudes, and leaned over talking to her for a while, and then pulled out his handkerchief, intending to rub his hands, and jerked his pipe out of his pocket with it. It took a lot of explaining, but he thought he'd managed it all right, and then he came out into the porch, and wanted to know what I meant by trying to make a fool of him.

I couldn't understand what he was trying to get at for a while, but gradually it dawned on me that it was my standing smoking in the doorway that he objected to. "As it happens," Gus told me, "It's the best thing you could have done. We both know what sort of man you are now." That hurt my feelings, and I decided I wouldn't go and ask Violet for any more dances.

Gus let one or two more go by, and then stalked confidently in for another. He asked Violet if she was engaged, and she fixed her eyes on a crack in the ceiling and said, in a voice that sounded as if she had a mouth full of hot potato, "I don't care to dance with you, Mr. Tomlins." Gus came out into the porch again, and spoilt the whole evening, as far as I was concerned. He said the next time I saw him interested in a girl, I was to keep away, and not come and deliberately 'put his pot on' the way I'd just done. I wasn't to come over to his place borrowing, and I was to leave him alone altogether. He didn't want to know me. He remained cool and distant for nearly a week, and then it got near his ploughing time, and he wanted to borrow a horse, so he gradually thawed. He told the people about that I was a dangerous man to have anything to do with. I meant well

Violet Again

at heart, but I had an unfortunate habit of saying the wrong things always, and giving people the wrong impression about things.

The day after he met Violet in town, accompanied by a tall man smoking a meerschaum, he buried the hatchet. He came over that night and sat smoking before the fire, with his dirty boots stuck up on my mantel shelf.

"You know Mark," he said, "If I hadn't understood women pretty well, that girl might have made a proper fool of me. If I hadn't seen through her, and dropped her, she might even have tried to stop me from smoking. And look at the way she tried to get you and I quarrelling."

Mowing Our Hay

Just before the hay-making season commenced, the second year Gus Tomlins and I were farming, Gus came over to my bach and said, "Slip over to tea tonight Mark, I want to have a good yarn with you."

"Why not come here to tea?" I asked. I knew Gus well enough by that time not to feel unduly honoured by the invite. If I do slip over to his place for a meal, I've generally got to nip back and get some of my own tea, or bread, or something.

"Come over to my place," said Gus. "I've got something important to show you."

After I'd finished milking I went across. Gus had just got inside, and was busy pouring kerosene into the fireplace.

"Take a rest," he commanded, "and I'll show you how to cook a feed in quick time." He rescued the frying pan from the corner where the cats were snoozing; gave it a perfunctory swill out with cold water — in honour of my visit, I presume — and filled it with sausages.

Just before this we had a week's wet weather, and hanging across the fireplace by a string were about twenty pairs of damp socks. Two or three times the sausages caught fire, and every time this happened Gus would pull out the pan with a jerk, and dislodge a sock or two.

I didn't mind that, although one fell in the pot of hot water, and had to be fished out with a fork, but I did object when he caught a particularly clammy-looking sock on the sausages.

"You're a queer chap," said Gus, heaving the greasy sock at my dog in the doorway as he spoke.

"It hardly touched them, and yet you fly off as if it were fried socks I was offering you."

After Gus had made a hearty meal — I was off my tucker a bit — he explained why he had invited me over.

Mowing Our Hay

"Look here Mark," he commenced. "There's an almost new mower in town that can be bought for £6. My idea is, that instead of paying old Harry Johns six bob an acre to mow all our hay, we club in together and buy it."

I didn't know Gus half as well then as I do now, so I considered the idea.

He put the proposition so well that it sounded like a real good thing. He was to take charge of the machine, as he knew just about all there was to know about mowing machines, while I was to lend my horse, and do all the running about that should be required.

"Not that there will be any," added Gus, "because properly handled, a mower is the sweetest running machine made."

Next day we slipped into town in my dray and purchased the 'snip', and brought it home.

We unloaded it at Gus's place, so that he could give it a thorough overhaul before we started to use it.

"All she wants," explained Gus, "is tightening up here and there, and plenty of oil."

It was decided to cut my six acres of hay first, so as soon as Gus pronounced the machine in working order, I took my horse over to him and we prepared to make a start. The first thing we found we hadn't got was a proper pole harness, but Gus got over that by making canvas straps out of an old cow cover.

"See what it is to have brains?" he pointed out.

He hopped onto the seat and flicked old Bloss with the rein, and she jumped into her collar and broke the rotten old canvas strap before old Darky had woke up enough to know they were under way.

The pole dug into the ground, and Gus climbed down and spoke severely to Darky.

After we had made a new strap, Gus took his seat again and said, "take that waddy Mark, and if they don't start off together fetch the slowest a good clip." He clicked and shook the reins, and Darky, remembering what Gus had said to him, hopped off the mark and almost wrecked our new machine before we'd started.

After that we got a piece of green hide, and made the pole fast to their collars properly. We got out into my paddock safely, although I didn't care about the way the two horses were behaving, but Gus said that was all right, he'd soon show them. Neither horse had done any pole work before, and Bloss was trying to move sideways like a crab, while old Darky looked as if he'd like to kick the stuffing out of the whole turnout.

"Follow me round a couple of times," directed Gus, "and then you can buzz off and wash your cans, and then wash mine."

I followed him round as ordered. Every two or three yards the knife would clog, and I would have to clear it while Gus looked on and directed.

"The whole trouble Mark," explained he, "is the two horses. They won't start off together."

That did seem to be the trouble. As soon as Gus started them off, Bloss would jump into her collar and pull the machine a yard or two by herself. Just as she decided it was a false alarm and stopped, the swinglebar would catch old Darky across the hocks and start him off. By the time both horses were pulling together the knife would be clogged again.

After I'd nearly lost a hand clearing the grass from the teeth, through Gus forgetting to throw the machine out of gear, we had a few words.

"Get out of the way," yelled Gus, losing his temper. "I'll make them pull together." He doubled the bight of reins in his hands and lammed both horses as hard as he could, and they broke into a gallop. My hay paddock was on a hillside, and I had to stand and watch the picnic. They galloped all out up the hill first, took a wide turn, and then came charging down again, with Gus perched on the seat, swinging the reins round and raving like a maniac.

He had omitted to raise the knife or throw it out of gear, and it dragged through the long grass, just occasionally letting out a b-r-r-r-r-r as it worked for a second or two before reclogging.

"I'll teach them," bellowed Gus, as he flew past me and made another wide circle.

Mowing Our Hay

Three times round the paddock, taking a different path each time, and both horses were in a lather. Then Gus pulled them in to a trot and drew up to the starting point again.

"That's the way to teach them who's boss," he remarked complacently. "Now they'll pull together, I bet."

"Yes," said I coldly. "And look at my hay. Nice mess, isn't it?"

"Pooh!" said Gus, "that's nothing. Once I get started I'll mow all that as close as a lawn."

He hopped off his seat, to oil the works, and we both put in a quarter of an hour following his tracks, hunting for the oil can.

"Now, if you'd kept your eyes open, when I was straightening up those two horses," grumbled Gus, after he had found it, "you'd have seen it fall off."

He oiled up carefully, making the interesting discovery as he did so that the tool box was open and all the tools missing.

"Never mind, I'll find them as I do the paddock," he said, "and it's hardly likely I'll need them before I've finished."

He climbed into his seat again and, shaking the reins, shouted "Giddap!" The horses answered at once, but the knife refused to chatter.

"That's funny," said Gus. "Clear the teeth, Mark."

I cleared the teeth cautiously, and he backed the mower and tried again. Then he jumped off his seat and we raised the knife and investigated. It was snapped in half about half way along, and the bearing of the driving rod was broken off as well.

"Not so funny after all," remarked I.

"Now, what could have done that?" puzzled Gus, scratching his head.

I suggested that dragging the knife through my hay at full gallop with the teeth all clogged might have been responsible.

"Don't be a fool," said Gus. "I've seen mowers cut through fencing wire, let alone a thin crop of hay like this."

Until Gus alluded to my crop in that tone I'd been under the impression it was fairly good.

"Well, what are you going to do now?" I asked.

"Me!" exclaimed Gus. "I don't do the running round. That's your job."

"Right oh!" said I. "Take old Bloss out and I'll slip into town and get a new knife."

We had to borrow a spanner from a neighbour before we could unslip the broken driving rod, and then I took the parts into town and had them replaced.

Next day Gus made a fresh start, and everything went smoothly for two rounds. He pointed out why the machine had refused to work the day before. Evidently the knife, being an old one, was too worn out to cut properly, hence the clogging.

"D'you know this Mark," he turned to shout, as he was going up the hill, with me following behind. "It's a darn good job that knife snapped with us as it did. If it hadn't, we'd have had continual trouble with it, and now we can go ahead all the season without a hitch."

Clang! Bang! "Whoa!"

The machine stopped with a screeching noise, and Gus hopped out to investigate.

It was one of the spanners that had shaken out of the tool box the day before.

"They might be able to cut through fencing wire," remarked I, "but they seem to jib on steel spanners."

"Humph," grunted Gus. "One thing, Mark, we don't have to tear off and borrow a spanner this time."

He proceeded to open out the newly found tool as he spoke, and we removed the broken knife with it. I slipped into town again, only to discover when I got there that it was half-holiday, and all the shops closed.

That hurt worse than anything, and I decided to give Gus a piece of my mind for not remembering it and telling me.

For the next two days Gus filled in time pottering about the mower with all the tools in the district that we could borrow. I was getting about fed up with it. About every other person I met down at the factory each morning had something smart to say about it.

Arty Wilcox worked off a stale joke on me. He said, "What's your opinion about this new 'auto' that's come out Mark?"

I said, "What new 'auto' Arty?"

Mowing Our Hay

"That auto mow grass Gus Tomlins has at your place," replied Arty.

Every fool laughed as if it were funny, and I went home and told Gus to either cut my hay or take the old derelict away, and let me hire a real mower.

"Don't get snappy," said Gus. "I've found out what's wrong now, and fixed it, so your hay will come down today without fail."

I helped him to harness up, and he made a start. Something was still a little out of place, and the knife gave the same old trouble, refusing to work.

The only time it shaped anything like at all was when my new pup was standing in front of it sniffing at Bloss's heels. I paid Black Joe, the drover, two pounds for that pup, so as to ensure having a good cattle dog for next season, and after I had carried him home and put him out of his misery, I slipped straight down to see old Harry Johns.

Harry said, "Yes, I'm going out mowing this year Mark, but it will be ten bob an acre to do that paddock of yours, it's messed so much."

"Come straight up," replied I.

As soon as Gus spotted Harry driving into the field he got his feelings hurt, and took our mower out on to the road.

"If I'm mowing a paddock," said Gus, "I like to be left alone to do it. I don't expect to see every man in the district with a machine coming along to help."

Harry knocked down the crop that day, and two days later, just as it was ready to come in, the weather broke, and I had a fortnight's rain on it before I got it in. Gus said it served me right, if I'd left the job to him, it wouldn't have happened. I couldn't see his argument, unless he meant it wouldn't have been cut when the weather broke, and I don't think he meant it that way.

Our old mower stopped out on the side of the road for a week, and then Harry Johns offered me ten bob for my share of it.

"I've already bought Tomlins's half," he said.

Mark and Gus

I snapped the offer before he had time to change his mind.

"'Tisn't that it's any good much," explained Harry. "Only some of the spare parts might do for my machine."

Then he took it home, straightened a couple of combs or teeth, or whatever they call them, and mowed 220 acres with it, without a single hitch or breakdown.

After that I lost a lot of my faith in Gus Tomlins.

The End

www.ingramcontent.com/pod-product-compliance
Lightning Source LLC
Chambersburg PA
CBHW051710040426
42446CB00008B/815